THE HERALD DIARY

A Quacking Good Read

THE HERALD DIARY

A Quacking Good Read

Ken Smith

BLACK & WHITE PUBLISHING

First published 2019
by Black & White Publishing Ltd
Nautical House, 104 Commercial Street
Edinburgh, EH6 6NF

1 3 5 7 9 10 8 6 4 2   19 20 21 22

ISBN: 978 1 78530 266 4

A CIP catalogue record for this book is available from the British Library.

Typeset by Iolaire Typography, Newtonmore
Printed and bound by CPI Group (UK) Ltd, Croydon, CR0 4YY

Contents

Introduction   vii

1. No Mean City   1
2. With All My Heart   17
3. All in a Day's Work   27
4. Down the Pub   39
5. Gets Our Vote   49
6. Fly Guys   61
7. The Way They Tell Them   78
8. Being Childish   97
9. Saved by the Bell   107
10. Off to Yoonie   116
11. A Senior Moment   122
12. It's the Law   129
13. From the Heart   137
14. Keeping It Healthy   142
15. Shop Till You Drop   149
16. Transports of Delight   156
17. Chosen at Random   168
18. Technically Speaking   173
19. Gone But Not Forgotten   179
20. A Sporting Chance   194

Introduction

"If you didn't laugh, you'd cry," is the age-old phrase much repeated across the country in the last year as folk tried to understand Brexit, global warming and an American President who even his friends would describe as unpredictable.

Scotland, the country that has brought to people's attention comedians such as Billy Connolly, Kevin Bridges, Chic Murray and Stanley Baxter, knows all about laughing at adversity – how else could you cope with Scottish weather, Scottish politicians and the Scotland football team?

Fortunately, Scots, when they hear a good story, often phone or email The Diary column of the country's best-selling quality newspaper *The Herald* to delight and entertain its readers daily.

And the very best stories are brought together in this popular annual compilation which will continue to bring a smile to folk trying to look on the bright side of life.

1

No Mean City

The Diary welcomes stories from all over the world, but we do have a special affection for those stories from Glasgow, which we often think sum up the great city better than anything else.

GLASGOW private hire drivers will have to sit a test on their English language skills and their knowledge of the city if new measures are agreed by Glasgow City Council's licensing committee. Mind you, there can be language problems even if the driver is a native-born Glaswegian. A reader once told us he was in a Glasgow taxi with a colleague from London who was having difficulty opening the door. She seemed even more perplexed when the driver helpfully told her: "Pullrahonnelhen."

JUST another weekend in Glasgow. Panto star and comedian Johnny Mac passed on this observation from the city's West End: "Kelvingrove Park benches – a family enjoying a picnic of hummus and roast vegetables at one, while on another bench a guy is drinking a bottle of Buckfast while on the phone to his mate saying, 'No I can't go back to Nicola's flat – I'm just oot some burd's hoose and I've no showered.'"

A GLASGOW reader swears to us he heard a young woman in the town tell her male pal: "Have you seen my cat tattoo?" and he replied: "How does it hold the needle?"

A VIGNETTE from Glasgow's Buchanan Street where a Milngavie reader watched a young chap go over to a mendicant sitting on the street and ask him if he could buy him something to eat.

The supplicant replied: "Aye, great! A chicken and bacon sandwich out of Sainsbury's – and a medium-sized strawberry milkshake, mate. Okeydokey?" This proved too much for the Good Samaritan who told him: "Have you ever heard the expression 'Beggars can't be choosers'?" and walked on.

JUST a vignette from the streets of Partick on a Friday evening. A female jogger is running on the spot at the traffic lights on Dumbarton Road waiting for them to change so she can cross. A chap in a T-shirt, which appears to be attempting to keep his five bellies under control, is outside the Rosevale Bar with his mate having a fag. "Nice boobs, hen," he tells the runner, although he might not have used the word boobs. As the lights change, she replies: "Likewise, mate," and heads off as Smoker's pal laughs in his face.

A READER in Australia declared: "I saw a car in Sydney with a sticker on the back window saying, 'I Miss Glasgow.' So, I smashed a window, nicked his radio, then left a note stating, 'Hope this helps.'"

ANOTHER Australian reader once told us: "On a visit home to Scotland we stopped in Stonehaven for lunch. When we asked what the soup was, everyone thought our Glaswegian waitress replied, 'Thai soup.' I wondered aloud whether it might be too spicy for our two-year-old daughter, but was assured it was not by the puzzled girl. Only then did it dawn on me that she was talking about 'tattie soup', complete with glottal stop."

A GLASGOW reader heard an auld fella on his bus into town discussing with his pal the current fashion to have tattoos, and he came out with the memorable line: "I mean, when I was young you could make out what they were – a heart or a flower or something. But now some o' they young folk's arms look like the inside of your old school desk's lid."

A READER in London declares: "When I moved down south from Glasgow, I told everyone that my nickname at school was 'Scarface'. I never explained it was because I was brilliant at knitting."

ANOTHER London reader told us: "There was one other Scot working in my office who became a good pal, but unfortunately he moved back to Glasgow. Occasionally folk would ask me in the pub, 'Where's your pal Crawford?' I would shake my head and tell them, 'He's gone to a better place.' They express their condolences until I explain that Glasgow really is a better bet than London these days."

SAW one of these pointless social media questions where someone asked: "If I were to break into your house and steal what is on top of your refrigerator, what am I getting?" A Jerry Edwards from Glasgow merely replied: "Dust. Help yourself."

AH, Glasgow life. A vignette from stand-up Janey Godley who explains: "Got woke up with the bin men at 8 a.m. They have a new wee guy on the squad whose voice hasn't broken yet, and he was shouting and swearing 'bants' to impress the gang – like a really nervous sweary Kate Bush, if Kate Bush was from Govan."

A GLASGOW reader swears he heard a young woman in his pub the other night declare: "I'm no longer on Facebook," and her pal replying: "So how do you know when it's your birthday?" It reminds us of a colleague who felt the need to tell us: "Did you know that the most prolific user on Facebook has died? We won't see the likes of him again."

THE announcement that *The Buteman* newspaper is to close reminds us of a reader of The Diary who sent us the story from the paper of the countryside ranger who went to check an eight-foot-long bird hide at Ascog Loch which had been built to help twitchers spot the rare birds that stop off on Bute on their annual migrations. Inside, he found a family of four from Glasgow who were having a holiday in it, complete with food, milk, newspapers . . . and a fold-up settee.

MARRIED life can be tricky. A Glasgow reader heard a chap in his local pub explain to his pals: "The dog ran in from the garden with its mucky paws leaving a trail over the living-room carpet. 'Do something!' shouted the wife. Apparently reaching for my mobile phone to record a film of it wasn't what she had in mind."

AND a reader once explained: "My wife planted a few shrubs of herbs in our wee back garden. She then asked me, 'Could you nip out and cut some parsley for me, please?' Displaying my ignorance of such Jamie Oliver-type knowledge I said,

'How will I know which one is parsley?' She replied, 'It's the one to the right of the mint.'"

WE asked about conversations and events that can only happen in Glasgow. A reader passes on a message he read on social media from a young Celtic supporter who stated: "One of the guys ah work with is a Rangers fan, but brand new. He had a stroke and was in a coma for a few days. Daft Kev, who's a Celtic fan, sent him a card saying, 'Rab, you've been in a coma for three years. Celtic got ten in a row! Get it up ye."

A GLASGOW reader swears he heard a young woman criticising her pal for drinking too much and the pal defending herself by saying: "What's wrong with fancying a man in a uniform?" But her pal replied: "Honey, he was a statue of a pilot in a travel agent's doorway."

ONLY in Glasgow . . . Ian Watson tells us his Glaswegian cousin and wife, long exiled in the USA, had returned to celebrate their 50th wedding anniversary in Mackintosh at the Willow on Sauchiehall Street.

Says Ian: "It being a sunny Saturday afternoon the professional photographer hired to capture the occasion assembled the guests outside. With cameras and huge lenses hanging off each shoulder she was lining up one group in front of the Art Nouveau frontage when she felt a tap on her shoulder followed by, 'Gie's yer camera, hen, and I'll take one of youse all.'"

AS others sees us: a magazine in Houston, Texas, the *Houstonia*, started a travel piece about Glasgow with the statement: "Googling 'Glasgow', the results are sobering. 'Pregnant woman attacked and robbed in Glasgow.' And 'Glasgow gangland wars have scarred city with stabbings, shootings and murder.' Scotland's largest city has a bit of a reputation."

However, the author had a good time when he visited the city so he then adds the memorable line: "Don't join a gang or precipitate a bar fight, and you should be fine."

OUR tales of unpretentious Glasgow shops remind Hilary Shearer: "We returned to Glasgow from living in the Netherlands and, wishing to continue with our new-found sophistication, decided to add some kirsch to a cheese fondue one evening – it was the 1970s after all. Husband duly set forth to acquire kirsch at the nearest off-licence, only to have the wee wifie behind the counter peer up at him and enquire, 'Who dae you think you are, James Bond?'"

SOME of our stories about the Glasgow Subway have referred to its diminutive size. As Douglas Kirkham tells us: "When I was wee, my big brother took me for my first subway trip. I couldn't wait to get home to tell my mum I was on a train that went up a close."

A STRUCTURAL engineer from south of the Border, newly arrived in Glasgow, was struggling to persuade local workmen to remove material from a site. After ranting at length, he concluded by demanding to know when, precisely, the material would be shifted. The bored foreman answered: "Ah've no' got a scooby, pal." To which the exasperated chap from England pleaded: "Well, go get one. Hire a Scooby if you have to. Just get this stuff removed."

THINGS you only hear in Glasgow's West End, continued. A reader tells us her friend in Kirklee was explaining that she had a visit from the grandchildren over the Easter weekend. She said that one of the lads was a bit shy and then used the memorable phrase: "He spent most of the afternoon hiding under the chaise longue."

OUR story about the hen party downing pints at Glasgow Airport at 6.45 a.m. reminded Douglas Hutchison in Kilcreggan: "When Glasgow and Edinburgh Airports were owned by the same company, they were benchmarked against each other in terms of customer satisfaction, by means of surveys. Edinburgh apparently always performed badly as the researchers would interview bleary-eyed businesspeople heading to London on the first shuttle and be given short shrift. In contrast, at Glasgow, researchers would be welcomed by happy holidaymakers and invited to join them for a pint in the bar. Always scored higher marks."

WE ran stories of the moon landing, but a reader went further by reminding us of the Moon nightclub on Sauchiehall Street – it was after my time as I knew it as the White Elephant. Anyway, although it has closed, you can still read reviews of it on Yelp, where a woman named Adele left the memorable comment: "Worst nightclub around. The clientele was a sleazy mix of lecherous old men and miniskirt-wearing minors, who seemed to be getting along famously. When I was approached and asked if I had a boyfriend by a man older than my dad, I turned on my heel and left immediately."

OUR Glasgow nightclub story about old men chasing young women reminds a reader of the city's Savoy disco where the DJ, without really thinking this through, announced that the next record "is for one of our long-term regulars, Jeannie, who is celebrating her 18th birthday tonight".

WE liked the brutal honesty of Castlemilk singer-songwriter Gerry Cinnamon whose shows are selling out fast because of a recent surge in popularity. He has told fans: "If you're selling my tickets and you're sound, please resell them on the Twickets app at face value. If you're an old-school tout outside the show making a £20 skin, then do what you do. If you're selling tickets for £200 to £300, do me a favour and only sell them in person so people can meet you and punch your face in."

WE can just imagine the conversation as young Amna was telling her pals on social media about returning to Glasgow. Said Amna: "I was helping out at my dad's shop when a customer asked, 'Oh, are ye wan ay the weans?' I replied, 'Aye, just helping out for a wee bit the day.' Said the customer, 'Which wan are ye again? The teacher? Or the wan who never visits?'"

OUR attention is drawn to the Italian newspaper *La Stampa*, which was writing about Glasgow. We enjoyed the bit about the Italian reporter arriving at Central Station and calling an Uber taxi. The driver told him that he had been an airport driver for 20 years, but had been told by a pal about this new thing called Uber. He feared that it would ruin the taxi trade so he sold his licence just before Uber arrived here. When the Italian visitor asked who he had sold the licence to, he laughed and replied: "The brother-in-law."

THE *Herald* reported that ATMs are disappearing from our high streets at an alarming rate. I remember our old chum Tom Shields telling readers about a beggar who stood at the ATM outside Alldays in Great Western Road and who did not look a well man, ragged, red-eyed, shivering and shaking. He held out his hand to a well-dressed customer with his usual request for "spare change". The man replied: "I don't give money to beggars. Why don't you sell *The Big Issue?*" to which the beggar replied: "I regard this as more of a challenge." The bloke gave him a quid.

WE read that plans have been submitted for 250 flats to be built at the old Glasgow Meat Market on Duke Street. We were once told by John Sword who worked there of a bull that escaped from the abattoir and was eventually cornered in the backcourt of a Gallowgate tenement. After the animal was safely secured, a wee wummin went up to the chap who put it in the lorry and said: "Are you in charge?" Thinking he was about to get a wee hawf or somesuch from a grateful local he cheerily confirmed he was. "Well, it's my turn furra sterrs – so you can clean up," she said and handed him a mop and bucket.

WE read that 23 folk were barred from Glasgow libraries last year for crimes ranging from verbally abusing staff to using other people's library cards. It reminds us of the reader who told us about a chap years ago in Lanarkshire who was returning an overdue book who was told that the fine was five pence. The old chap offered up a five-pound note and said he had nothing smaller, so the librarian let him off. As he turned away from the counter he was about to sneeze, yanked a hankie out of his pocket, and spilled a load of change onto the library floor.

A GLASGOW reader tells us she was in a coffee shop in the city when a woman on her way out stopped another lady in the queue and told her: "That's a lovely perfume you are wearing, what is it?" The coffee buyer merely replied: "February *Vogue*, round about page 90."

A GLASGOW businessman tells us of a colleague, a chap careful with his money, who bragged about buying a flat in a more challenging district of Glasgow because it was so cheap. Unfortunately, his house was broken into and items stolen. Perhaps through hubris, he felt he should be compensated and was too imaginative financially in his subsequent insurance claim.

He then panicked when told an insurance adjuster was coming out to discuss his extravagant claims. His solution? When the adjuster called round, he stood at the door naked, stating he had just come out of the shower, and invited the chap in. The conversation only lasted a few minutes before the adjuster rapidly left.

The claim was met in full.

BIG day for Old Firm fans on Sunday. As Grace's Irish Sports Bar in Glasgow's Merchant City later explained on social media: "As always after a great day we have various items of lost property consisting of: three phones, ten jackets, two wallets, one pair of specs and a set of false teeth." We did like the false teeth reference, as it creates an image of a fan shouting so loud at the telly that their teeth flew out.

As one young Glasgow woman replied: "Sounds like our office Christmas night out."

OUR mention of stories that could only happen in Glasgow reminded John Gillick of being a teenager and seeing Rod Stewart and the Faces at Glasgow's Apollo where he athletically caught one of the footballs that Rod had kicked into the crowd.

Says John: "One of the stewards advised me to leave there and then as if I didn't someone was likely to relieve me of it. However, I stayed to watch the rest of the concert. At the end, as I made my way out, three older guys converged on me and blocked my exit. As I stood clutching the ball trying not to look afraid, the guy in the middle pointed to the ball and said, 'Did you catch that, wee man? How do you fancy playing in goals for us tomorrow?'"

A STORY in *The Herald* which mentioned the now-demolished Calderpark Zoo in Glasgow reminded Neil Dunn: "I was up in the Radio Clyde 'Eye in the Sky' in the 1980s with the late 'Captain' George Muir on a rare occasion when he carried passengers and there was not much traffic news to report. He scooted along to the zoo and hovered over the bear enclosure and we watched as said bear rose majestically and roared. Whether with greeting or annoyance we will never know."

TODAY'S piece of whimsy comes from a Glasgow reader who emails: "I replaced our couch with a trampoline. The wife hit the roof."

DOCTOR Duncan Sim tells us of the service he and a female colleague received in a Bridgeton cafe. Plonking down two cups of tea, the waitress informed her customers: "The sugar's in."

Duncan's colleague piped-up in protest: "But I don't take sugar." The waitress was not unduly distressed.

"Ach, jist dinnae stir it, hen," she said, and sauntered off.

WE recall the inexperienced theatregoers who settled into their seats at the Citizens Theatre to enjoy a performance of *Waiting for Godot*.

Rather spoiling the evening's entertainment, the bloke turned to his date before the curtain rose and whispered: "He willnae come, ye know. His name's no' in the programme."

2

With All My Heart

If ever there was an area that many Scotsmen struggle with it is their relationship with wives and partners. Some survive by smiling at adversity. Here are their latest stories.

TODAY'S daft gag comes from a reader who emails: "Bloke in the pub last night said he had asked his girlfriend if he was the only one she had ever been with. He said she confirmed that he was, then added: 'All the others were nines and tens.'"

WE received the thought-provoking comment from a Hyndland reader who emailed: "Nobody says, 'What are you going on about?' more than a man who knows exactly what you are going on about."

A GLASGOW reader swears to us he overheard a young woman in a coffee shop tease her mother by asking: "So when I came along, what was it you really wanted, a boy or a girl?" but the mother simply replied: "Thinking back to when you were conceived all I really wanted was a back rub."

ANOTHER Glasgow reader claimed he heard a woman in a coffee shop at the weekend tell her pal: "My husband paid for one of these DNA tests to find out your ancestry. I asked him if it confirmed that he was 60% sofa."

TRICKY things marriages. A reader phones to tell us: "The key to a successful marriage is letting things go. I've started with myself."

INEVITABLY there was a joke or two about the world's richest man, Amazon boss Jeff Bezos, splitting up from his wife. As TV presenter Richard Osman put it: "I see Amazon boss Jeff Bezos's wife is leaving him. With a neighbour, presumably."

WE are often sent pictures from readers exasperated at the large size of cardboard boxes that Amazon use to deliver quite modestly sized goods, so no doubt they will empathise with a reader who declared: "I just used three of my wife's Amazon delivery boxes to store all of my wife's Amazon delivery boxes."

MARRIED life, continued. Kent Graham muses: "How can my wife's hands not open a jar of pickles in the day, but become superhuman vice-grips at night when I want some covers?"

TODAY'S piece of daftness comes from a reader who emails: "Therapist, 'I think you have a phobia of marriage.

Do you know what the symptoms are?' Patient, 'Can't say I do.' Therapist, 'That's one of them.'"

A READER emails: "I have recently been employed as a night-watchman by a security firm owned by my ex-girlfriend. My wife is furious that I still carry a torch for her."

IT may not be that hot but the grass is still shooting up. As a Newton Mearns reader ruefully asks us: "Why is it so easy to immediately notice when my neighbour cuts his grass, but so hard to notice when my wife has had her hair cut?"

AN AYRSHIRE reader was in his golf club bar when he heard a fellow member announce: "My wife's giving me the silent treatment." "You're lucky," replied another member, "My wife gives me the speaking treatment."

ANOTHER Ayrshire reader tells us a retired chap at his local golf club let everyone in on a secret. "I write down fake chores on my to-do list then score them out so that when the wife comes home, she actually thinks I've done something," he declared.

MARRIED life, continued. An exasperated wife emails The Diary: "It takes my husband longer to choose a rental car online than it did for us to choose the names for our sons."

INTERESTING how married life develops. A reader tells us a chap at his golf club was explaining to fellow members: "The first time my wife left me for a few days to visit the grandchildren down south, she left me meals she had prepared in the freezer with dates on them explaining when I should eat them. This week when she went all I got was a list of recorded TV programmes that I was instructed not to watch until she got home."

WE dip into social media where folk have been sharing the funny things they do to annoy their partners. We liked the woman who admitted that when she drops her husband off at the station or anywhere where there is a crowd, she screams as he alights: "Get out of my car!" and quickly drives away.

A GLASGOW reader swears to us he heard a woman in a West End coffee shop tell her pal: "I've worked out that I'm paranoid and needy at the same time. I think people are talking about me – but not as much as I'd like."

WE hear from reader Sandy Lyall, who recalls: "My late father, a Church of Scotland minister in a country parish, annoyingly, when telephoning parishioners, would not immediately say who he was. This went on until he phoned one extremely attractive lady parishioner and when she asked who was calling, he replied that he had visited her, dined with her and even danced with her. Not having a clue who he was she asked, 'Have you slept with me?' After that scenario he changed his telephone approach."

THERE was the classic Diary story, when we were on a run of strange tales about Kilwinning, which claimed that a young Kilwinning chap proudly told his mum that he was marrying a virgin. But his mother replied: "Son, if she's no good enough for the boys in Kilwinning, then she's no good enough for you."

A GLASGOW reader said he had to smile when he heard a young chap up the bar tell his pals: "Whenever your girlfriend says to you, 'We need to talk,' why is it never about football?"

AN AYRSHIRE reader tells us: "A member of the golf club cheerily announced in the bar yesterday, 'My wife wanted me to try three new positions in the bedroom last night.' He then added, 'But after a lot of huffing and puffing she decided she wanted the dressing table to remain where it was.'"

A READER at a wedding of an optician friend said that the minister couldn't resist saying to the couple when they were taking their vows: "Do you, Karen, take David the optician to be your lawfully wedded husband, for better or worse? Better . . . or worse? Better . . . or worse?"

AH yes, wedding receptions, and a reader on Arran told of a friend arriving at a reception being held in a very expensive hotel carrying a beautifully wrapped present which she sat on the table. Only the most eagle-eyed spotted that it was in fact a carefully wrapped wine box from which she discreetly topped up her glass all evening, before disposing of the then empty box in the bin, leaving none of the hotel staff any the wiser.

TODAY'S piece of daftness comes from Paul Eggleston who declares: "It's more romantic to say 'bouquet' rather than 'bunch'. That's what I told my wife when I gave her a bouquet of bananas on our anniversary."

WHY DID THE
FLINTSTONES
CELEBRATE
CHRISTMAS

WE asked for your wedding gift stories, and a reader directs us to a wedding advice website where a young woman writes: "A lady I used to work with dropped by my house today to drop off our wedding gift. She opened her handbag and handed over six glass tumblers, not in a box or wrapped or anything. She then went on to tell me how thankful I should be as she had to 'down six vodkas' to steal these glasses from a restaurant she attended.

"I was so shocked and thought she was kidding – she wasn't. Do I send a thank you card for this?"

A GLASGOW reader claims he heard a woman on his bus into town tell her pal: "My husband would win gold in the

Lazy Olympics – if he could ever bother getting off his back-side to enter them."

THAT great Scottish actress Maureen Beattie is to appear in a trilogy of plays entitled *Interference*, which will be staged in the old Wills tobacco factory in Dennistoun. Maureen was once asked by our colleague Brian Beacom when she was not performing, and she replied: "Only when I'm asleep." She then gave an example of having an argument with a boy-friend at the time when she was appearing in a play about a couple splitting up. Her then-boyfriend halted her harangue to point out to her she was merely repeating lines from the play.

OUR stories suggesting that teenagers don't always think things through reminds a reader in Strathaven: "My wife asked our eldest to come home from school during the lunch break and let the dog out. Wife duly returned home later in the afternoon to discover dog in the garden and back door left wide open. Lesson learned re being more specific with instructions."

OH, and if we were suggesting that teenagers are not always the most helpful, we should also acknowledge that husbands can sometimes also fall into that category. As a reader emails to tell us: "My husband texted me to let me know that he had emptied the dishwasher while I was out. I responded:

Calm down, pet, if I texted every task I did, it would be a novel."

A FEMALE reader tells us: "It's pretty obvious that car designers are all men. Why isn't there a button on the dashboard you can press for 'It's only some shopping bags, for God's sake!' when the fasten-seatbelt pinger goes off."

A GLASGOW reader swears he heard a woman on the bus into town tell her pal: "My boyfriend's that thick that when he saw the sign 'built in antenna' on my portable TV he said he didn't know where that was."

A SCOT living in America who was heavy with child, informed us that she and her husband checked out the local hospital where the baby was due to be born, and discovered the facilities were more like a hotel. The birthing room had a spa bath, soft music and candles.

"What do you think?" she asked her husband. "It was a place like this," he replied, "that got us into this trouble in the first place."

3

All in a Day's Work

Even with the growing numbers of people who work from home, going into an office is still where many people spend a third of their day, chatting to colleagues, making cups of tea, even doing the occasional bit of work, and it's where many of their stories for The Diary suddenly spring up.

A GLASGOW reader tells us he and fellow staff at his office were dragooned into a meeting room for a talk by an inspirational speaker hired by the company for some reason. He liked how, when the speaker asked, "What inspires you to get up every day?" someone in the audience answered: "My bladder mostly."

A READER whose pal is known for his funny stories told him the other day: "My boss emailed me and said he was having to give a speech and could I tell him some jokes. I emailed him back and said I was very busy working, but would send him something later. He emailed me back saying, 'That's hilarious. Send some more.'"

A GLASGOW reader swears he heard a young man in the pub tell his pals: "Was interviewed by the police, but just said, 'No comment,' to every question. Thinking back, that's probably why I didn't get the job."

THE SNP is being attacked for giving local authorities powers to levy a tax on workplace parking spaces. It reminds us of the health and safety official at a large Glasgow factory giving a talk and asking staff: "Does anyone know the speed limit in the factory car park?"

A voice replied: "Depends. Do you mean coming in to work or leaving?"

WE asked about taking food to your office, and Jim Nicol in Lenzie recalls: "Back in the 1980s, as the office junior I was tasked with getting the morning roll order from the canteen for the other clerks. As a joke, I slipped a rubber band into a roll and bacon, buying a second as a replacement when my ruse was discovered. The clerkess chosen as my victim then wordlessly devoured the entire original roll without complaint. Eek!"

OUR stories of lunches in workplace fridges helped Russel Martin in Bearsden recall: "When I was an apprentice in a Clydeside marine engineering works, refrigerated storage facilities for lunchtime food were not a concept. Lunchtime 'pieces' or 'chits' as they were known, were often taken to work in a small tin. It was unwise to leave these lying around unattended. The more mischievous of the apprentices would remove the contents and drive a six-inch nail through the bottom and into the wooden work bench, before replacing everything. Attempting to remove one's 'chit boax' at lunchtime, to sit in a quiet corner, might lead to a sprained wrist trying to lift it."

TALKING of social media, we liked the comment from a young woman named Chloe who passes on: "Still canny get over the fact a boy at work said 'Y for young team' to a customer when he was spelling something out using the phonetic alphabet."

SAID BBC Scotland journalist Andrew Picken: "Someone at my mate's work said they were 'going to play devil's avocado on this one'. And nobody corrected him. Tremendous."

SAID a Jordanhill reader: "I was a trainee with British Rail years ago and was sent to Shields Electric Traction Depot on the south side of the city. In the messroom, used by drivers and maintenance staff, the depot manager had placed a sign above the sink stating, 'When the sink is full of teabags, please use the bin.' It was, and they had."

OUR tales of taking your own food into work remind John Milligan in Kilmarnock: "As a young fireman in the 1970s, when acting as kitchen assistant to an older, worldly-wise fireman in Kilmarnock Fire Station, the cook discovered he was one fish short for a fish and chips lunch. It didn't take long for him to stave off a potential mutiny. He produced a piece of white bread, cut off the crusts and shaped it to look like a fish fillet. With breadcrumbs applied it was deep fried along with the others and put out for lunch. The strange thing was, there were no complaints!"

OUR mention of firefighters cooking meals for their crew reminded one retired fireman: "Assisting the cook, I dropped an egg which broke under the kitchen table. Apologising to him, I said I'd put it in the bin, but he said he could still use it. I pointed out that the egg was now actually full of small bits of dirt and grit but he said, 'It'll be OK; they'll just think it's pepper.' We used the egg without any complaints."

A YOUNG woman who brought her baby into the Glasgow office where she worked, a few weeks after its birth, was telling her colleagues that the baby's birthday was nine months to the day after her husband's. "Next year I'd just get him a tie if I was you," said one of her colleagues.

TOUGH gig, being an actor and comedian. As Darren Connell, who plays the police-pestering Bobby on the BBC Scotland series *Scot Squad*, revealed: "Someone just asked me while I was in my local Asda buying hummus, 'Can you paint my fence for me? I know you do comedy stuff, so you won't get much work.' So, if my body gets found buried in someone's garden it's because I was painting a Random's fence."

WALKING down Glasgow's Byres Road the other day, Diary reader Carol Puthucheary heard a workman saying to his colleague, who was perhaps ill-advisedly sporting a pair of shorts: "The last time I saw a pair of legs like that, they were hingin' oot a nest!"

WE have carried a few stories about apprentices and the way they are treated at their work. Electrician Jason adds to the apprentice stories by passing on: "I was showing my apprentice how to do a fairly complex job. He stops me and says, 'I got it, it's not like you need to be a Science Rocketist to figure this out.'"

READER Joe Knox passes on: "I was at a Certificate of Professional Competence course for coach drivers last week and Robert the lecturer said he had fallen off a 50-foot ladder. After seeing our shocked faces, he added that he was pleased to say he was only on the bottom rung at the time."

AND for those who remember their American political history, business school psychologist Adam Grant in the States asked on social media: "What's the worst career advice you've ever received?" None other than Monica Lewinsky replied: "I was told an internship at the White House would be amazing on my resumé."

WE asked about spelling errors that should have been caught before sending, and Alan Russell in Edinburgh recalls: "An email sent around a global organisation on behalf of a department head called Angus. Unfortunately spellcheck didn't recognise the good Scottish name and omitted the 'g' from his name at the end of the missive. It didn't help matters that the Angus in question had a permanently rather puckered up expression."

WRITER David Barnett also asks: "What's the worst typing mistake in an email you spotted immediately after hitting send? I think mine has to be, 'I appreciate that you're very busty.'"

STEPHEN Henson tells us about a family friend who is an air steward arriving back at Glasgow from a flight very late at night.

Driving home to Ayrshire in the wee small hours she missed a bend on a country road and ended up in a muddy field in the pitch black, unharmed but shaken.

Says Stephen: "She made her way back to the road to flag down assistance. You can imagine the horrified look on the face of a local farmer she stopped who suddenly saw in his headlights a bedraggled, muddy air hostess in full uniform staggering out of a field. He flew out of the car in a blind panic shouting 'Where's the plane crashed? Where's the plane crashed?'"

A RECENTLY retired lawyer phones to tell us: "I still think back to the first trial I took as a young solicitor. After winning I rushed back to the office, charged in, and declared loudly, 'Justice prevailed!' My boss without even looking up replied: "Ah well, we can always think about an appeal."

BOB Mackie reminds us of the old HMS *Carrick* which was tied up on the Clyde in Glasgow near the High Court and was used as a club by the Royal Navy Volunteer Reserve. It was a bit posh and had quite high standards, evidenced by the fact I was only invited on it once.

Anyway, Bob recalls: "A chap in the RNVR who also worked in Yarrows came into work one morning where he was observed pulling at his ears and nose, creating something of a scene and complaining of the bends.

"He was asked what the trouble was and he said he had been diving at the weekend inspecting the hull of HMS *Carrick*. It was gently pointed out to him that if he had waited till low tide, he could have inspected the hull of the *Carrick* in his wellies."

SARCASM doesn't always work, it seems. As one worker in an office environment passes on: "I have worked with my new co-worker for almost a half hour now. It turns out that she's married so I asked her if her husband is deaf, but she hasn't stopped talking long enough to hear the question."

I KNEW I shouldn't have looked up, but I'm trapped by a colleague who tells me: "Only ten minutes into my semaphore course and I was already starting to flag."

TELEPHONE misunderstandings, continued. Says Andrew Lothian: "I took a call for a work colleague from a company whose name I didn't quite catch, though they were clearly local to the Edinburgh area. 'Who were they and what did they want?' she enquired. 'Not sure – something about an order for goats' cheese,' I replied. Calling them back, the phone was indeed answered 'Glentana Goats' Cheese.'

"After a short conversation, apparently at cross purposes, she came over to tell me it was an airport transfer service with no goats' cheese on offer. Seems that the receptionist used her best Edinburgh brogue to declare, 'Glentana Coach-ees!'"

GOOD to read in *The Herald* that although *The Buteman* newspaper is closing, the publishers of the *Dunoon Observer* and *Argyllshire Standard* have stepped in to fill the gap by launching *The Isle of Bute News*.

A reader recalling the old days of *The Buteman* admits it may have been a bit parochial at times as he recalled the front-page headline which declared: "Peace in Ireland a threat to Scottish tourism".

HOW to deal with the insincerity of bosses. A Glasgow reader tells us her boss came over to the person at the next desk in her office and said: "Sorry, are you in the middle of lunch?" The girl merely replied: "No, I just like holding sandwiches."

THERE are things many of us do, not realising that we are not alone in doing them. As Dan Regan admits: "When you are using your mobile phone and the person you are speaking to says, 'You're breaking up,' so you tell them, 'Hold on.' You then do absolutely nothing and a few seconds later ask, 'How's that?'"

OUR tale of the worker at Weir's of Cathcart giving out haircuts in company time reminds a former worker there of the amateur barber, who tells us that the chap would carry out his hairdressing in one of the company toilets with the customer sitting on the loo.

He added: "When a new employee looked under the closet door, concerned as it was always 'engaged', only to view two pairs of shoes facing each other, he reported what he thought was another activity entirely to management."

OUR story of the girl telling the astrophysicist that she was a Gemini reminded Archibald Crichton: "I was in Northern Ireland at a party once and was introduced to a young lady from New Zealand who told me she was a Libra. I went on to meet her husband who said he was a builder and that his wife worked for him on site. New Zealand accents!"

THE news stories about refugees in France sneaking on board British-bound lorries at ferry terminals reminds us of the Wishaw lorry driver who once told us that he was in the queue for the Channel ferry in France when a character waving a fistful of euros offered the cash in return for allowing immigrants to slip aboard his trailer.

Our man told him to beat it, but at that an Irish driver walked up, took the money, and undid the ties on the canvas sides of the truck next to the Wishaw driver, and the waiting travellers eagerly jumped aboard. The Irishman then pocketed the money and jumped in the cab of his lorry – which was further down the queue from the one he undid.

4

Down the Pub

As someone once observed: "Most of my best stories begin with having a pint. They very rarely begin with me having a salad." And so, many of our favourite Diary stories begin with having a pint.

A GLASGOW reader tells us a regular came into his pub the other night and announced: "Was in the bank where the wummin said my account was overdrawn. So I told her, 'And so's yer eyebrows, but you don't see me making a fuss about it.'"

A READER phones to tell us: "Thank goodness that's the amateur drinkers gone from our pubs for another year." When I ask what had upset him, he explains: "I was standing behind a lad at the bar who looked at the 80 Shilling India Pale Ale with its 80/- sign and asked for a pint of "Eighty slash dash."

OUR mention of that redoubtable Barras pub, the Sarry Heid, reminds Ninian Fergus: "Years ago I dropped into the Sarry Heid on my way to see Hibs play Celtic along the way.

"After no time an elderly gentleman sat down opposite me, and asked if I could spare some money so he could buy a drink. I duly obliged, and he told me he was down on his luck, just having returned from a spell in London. I asked him what he had been doing down there. 'Time,' he replied."

JAMES Thomson from Jordanhill was sweating it out in the heat of London at the weekend and tells us: "While waiting for an underground train I noticed on the wall that there was a poster for a leading tonic brand. Its caption was 'If three-quarters of your drink is the mixer, mix with the best.' Another traveller was reading this and said in a loud Scottish voice, 'If three-quarters of your drink is the mixer, I'd pour your drink again.'"

SYMPATHY goes out to the staff at Jamie Oliver's restaurant in Glasgow who have abruptly lost their jobs with the company going into administration. Reader Roy Ingram in Bearsden recalls: "Years ago I visited the restaurant in George Square, and was intrigued to see there was wild rabbit in the menu. 'How wild was the rabbit?' I asked the waitress. 'Absolutely furious,' she replied."

THE Forty Nine Wine & Spirit Club is for folk in the licensed trade to get to know more about the fine wines and spirits they serve. It is named after one of the finest years for claret and also the age limit of members – which was quietly dropped when all the founding members approached 49.

At their May lunch in Glasgow guest speaker, retired police officer Bobby Shaw, told them: "I was in a pub in Greenock where I asked, 'Do you have access to wi-fi?' But the barman replied, 'Ah don't even have access to ma weans.'"

WE were in a bar on St Patrick's Day, when an Irish customer asked for a Jameson's with water. When he sipped it, he asked the barman: "Which did you put in first?" "The whiskey," said the puzzled barman. "Ah well, no doubt I'll get to it eventually," the customer replied.

FOOTBALL players becoming publicans is still a thing, it seems. Former internationalist Steve Archibald mentioned on social media meeting ex-Hibs teammate Paul Kane and remarking what a nice guy he is. Author Irvine Welsh mentioned that Paul is now running a pub then reminisced: "He pulled me out of a brawl in Maribor into a secluded basement bar. When he bought us triple vodkas, I knew he was serious about not getting involved 'cause he's a notorious tightwad."

Hibs fan Alana Massie added: "Good guy, always made me feel welcome at the Four In Hand, although he did start charging everyone a pound to plug our own chargers in if we charged our phone. I had been going in for years and thought the barmaid was joking, but nope."

TODAY'S piece of daftness comes from a Partick reader who tells us about a very upmarket gastropub he recently dined in and finished his peroration with: "It was so posh that at the end of the meal I felt I had to ask for the William."

A READER tells us he heard a young chap in his local pub discussing a fellow pal with his friends and declaring: "He's that thick, if you started telling him a knock-knock joke he'd interrupt to say he thought there was someone at the door."

A READER in a Glasgow pub heard a group of younger customers discussing the TV licence, with one chap declaring he didn't have one and then adding: "I did get a letter from the licensing people at my flat which was addressed to 'Present Occupier'. I sent it back saying there was no one of that name currently residing there."

OUR stories about the legendary comedian Chic Murray vary from his gags to stories about meeting him, usually in Glasgow's West End where he lived for a while.

As Donald Macaskill recalls: "I was standing in a Byres Road hostelry with friends when Chic Murray hove to and immediately commenced a vigorous knees-up exercise. Responding to a quizzical look, he ceased, pointed downwards at a blotch on the otherwise pristine pub floor and said, 'Spot, running thereon,' and resumed his efforts. It all seemed quite logical at the time."

PUB yarns about dogs included the toper who declared: "The council wants to ban Pitbull terriers from the streets, but they're having problems identifying which dogs are Pitbulls. But I don't see what the problem is. If they've got short legs, square shoulders and an aggressive temperament – then the dog with them is probably a Pitbull."

And in another pub a drinker explained: "Dogs are tough. When I went home last night, I interrogated our dog for over an hour, but he still wouldn't tell me who's a good boy."

A GLASGOW reader tells us he was in his local the other night where folk were discussing the scariest thing they had ever done, with some talking about charity skydives and swimming with sharks. One toper, who was struggling to come up with anything, eventually blurted out: "I sneezed violently while crossing two lanes to leave the M77 at Kinning Park in the rush hour. I'm telling you, that was pretty scary."

OUR attempt to find the oldest pub in Scotland brings forth the claim from Jim Cook in Airdrie that the town's Wayside Tavern in Chapel Street is so old it is even mentioned in the Bible. Yes, Matthew 13:4 reads, "And some fell by the Wayside."

RESTAURANT disasters, continued. Says a reader: "When a fellow student was an English assistant in Germany for a year, he got his tongue in a fankle and instead of ordering *ein Kännchen Kaffee* – a pot of coffee – he ordered *ein Kaninchen*, which means a rabbit. The waiter told him that unfortunately they were only serving coffee in squirrels that day. And they say the Germans don't have a sense of humour!"

AND moving from restaurants to pubs, Brian Chrystal recalls: "In Sloan's bar in the 1970s we were joined by a friend just back from London. Resplendent in his trendy white suit he ordered four pints of lager. Betty the barmaid came back with just two. 'Excuse me,' says he, 'I asked for four pints.' 'Awfy sorry, son,' says Betty, 'Ah couldny hear ye fur yer suit.'"

WE asked about your restaurant mistakes, and Derek Miller in Torrance confesses: "More of a pub mistake than a restaurant one perhaps, but one evening, back in the 1980s, I sat at the bar of a poseurs' pub in Glasgow and ordered a trendy beer and some nuts. The barman advised that they only had pistachios, which were very sophisticated at that time. I sat crunching away, not wanting to lose face, but thinking they were the worst nuts of all time. 'Eh, you need to take them out of the shells, mate,' said mine host, trying unsuccessfully to stifle a snigger. Not my finest moment."

WE do like odd conversations on social media. Passing the time, someone asked folk what was the most embarrassing way they had hurt themselves. Ken in Liverpool replied: "Broke four ribs while ironing curtains. They were still hanging, and it was 3 a.m., and I was drunk, so it was mostly on me."

WE reckon a few folk can identify with Jo Diggity, who commented: "A waiter asked me 'Would you like to know the one thing on the menu we're out of tonight?' and I replied, 'No, no, I'll find it, thanks.'"

TODAY'S piece of daftness comes from Andrew Chamings who says: "Make parties more interesting by telling strangers, 'I want you to know that I personally have no problem with you being here.'"

ENTERTAINER Andy Cameron recounts: "As the barman puts down a pint of heavy the customer says, 'It's a bit cloudy, son,' to which the barman replies, 'Whit dae ye want for wan and sixpence, thunder and lightning?' The price of the beer indicates the age of the gag."

A GLASGOW reader heard a chap in his local come out with a random piece of information, which often happens in a pub. He declared: "Jehovah's Witnesses don't celebrate Hallowe'en." Our reader felt it was quite sharp of a fellow imbiber to reply: "Is that because they don't like random people coming to their door, uninvited?"

AND the growth in craft ales, especially India Pale Ale, reminded an Edinburgh reader of his grandfather telling the old gag: "Customer walks into a bar and says, 'Give me a beer.' 'Pale?' asks the barman. 'No, a glass will do fine,' replied the drinker."

ON THE subject of Glasgow restaurant staff, a Scotstoun reader in a West End Chinese restaurant asked what the difference was between the sweet and sour chicken on the menu and the sweet and sour chicken Hong Kong style listed further down. "One pound twenty-five," the waitress replied.

And a Glasgow reader had to smile when he took an English colleague up on business to an Indian restaurant where his colleague demanded to know if the curries were hot.

"Hot?" replied the waiter indignantly. "They're so hot they'll burn the a*** aff ye," which seemed to quieten the chap.

GLASGOW brewers Tennent's have opened a visitor centre, which reminds us of our favourite Tennent's story, which was the company rep going into a Gallowgate pub where the owner feared he might lose his licence as there had been a fight on the premises. The rep tried to reassure him that these things happen, but the owner added that the police had been called into the premises. Again the Tennent's rep said that it was a common event. "No' wi' horses it's no," replied the glum owner.

5

Gets Our Vote

We have the greatest admiration for people who can still find a joke amid the country's hair-raising political decisions of the last year.

WHEN Boris Johnson became Prime Minister, we recalled former PM David Cameron telling a Westminster Correspondents' Dinner: "I remember canvassing in a South Hampstead suburb with Boris during the London Mayoral election, and this very attractive, middle-aged woman came to the door and said, 'Boris! Lovely to see you! You are the father of one of my children!' The white hair stood up on end. He said, 'Oh, God, oh, cripes, oh. The media! What do you want? Is it money?' She said, 'No, you are the father of one of my children! I'm her maths teacher.'"

SOMETIMES you have to praise the honesty of politicians. At one election, the Tory candidate in Motherwell was asked in a local youth magazine interview, along with all the other candidates, what his links were with the town. He replied: "I have seen Motherwell Football Club playing on *Sportscene.*"

CAT lovers will totally understand what our health minister did, while non-cat lovers will shake their heads in disbelief. We simply pass on a magazine interview with Scottish Health Secretary Jeane Freeman when she was asked about her pet cat Tosca – a black cat with a malevolent glare if its picture is anything to go by – and what the most ridiculous thing she has ever done for her pet.

Jeane replied: "We headbutted a cat-flap. It took Tosca six months to work out the cat-flap – it was only after many weeks of personal demonstrations that she caught on."

HONEST, we have been trying to find some positive stories about Brexit. So we turn to Glasgow stand-up Janey Godley who explained at the weekend: "Last night at the Stand Comedy Club in Edinburgh a woman from the Netherlands who was in the front row of the audience agreed to post me over insulin and migraine tablets. So, in seven seconds I got a better Brexit deal than Theresa May did in two years."

FORMER Ayrshire MP Brian Donohoe has been reminiscing with us about local councillors and tells us: "There was one councillor giving a vote of thanks who paid a glowing appreciation to the women for the splendid purvey, but went on to give a special thanks to Mrs Simpson for the loan of her urinal for making the tea. Not a soul drank any from that moment on."

FED up with Britain coming last in Eurovision? A reader tries to comfort us by stating: "Don't worry, Britain. Next year we'll be smashing it in the World Trade Organisation Song Contest."

HOW can you turn the London Marathon into a political point? A reader tries by phoning to tell us: "It's disgusting that they're running the London Marathon again. They should just respect the result of the 2018 race. Traitors."

THE BBC reported that there has been some discussion at the Treasury about doing away with the penny coin, although traditionalists in the Tory government are likely to oppose it. It reminds us years ago of the trader at the Glasgow Barras who continuously shouted: "A cigarette lighter and a coat hanger for a penny." If you handed him the cash you were given a paper bag with a match and a nail in it.

NEWS from America where Democratic candidate hopeful and former vice-president Joe Biden has made a video to apologise for hugging women inappropriately in the past. A contact in the States, Todd Levin, remarks: "Sorry, but I don't buy this 'I gave inappropriate hugs because I'm from another generation' stuff. My mom is Joe Biden's age and I can't recall a single time she ever hugged me."

NIGEL Farage condemning Britain's Ambassador to America for telling the truth about Donald Trump reminds us of when Nigel was being touted as a possible replacement as ambassador. This was greeted by much derision with people debating who would be a better ambassador than Nigel Farage.

One suggestion we liked was: "A half-chewed jelly baby,

covered in pencil shavings, at the bottom of a playground bin." However, perhaps the most inspired suggestion was "Hillary Clinton".

TONY Blair's former spin doctor Alastair Campbell has announced he will not rejoin the Labour Party as it is no longer the party he once supported. It reminds us of when Alastair was on a train from Glasgow heading south when he observed on social media: "Too many Scottish Manchester United fans on train. English Premier League has been bad for Scottish football."

Within minutes someone replied: "So has Scottish football."

ALL this talk of politicians and their illegal drug habits reminds us of when Scottish LibDems leader Willie Rennie was asked about his indiscretions and he conceded that he had smoked cannabis while a student at university. "Do you still use it now?" he was then asked. "It might look like it, but I don't," he replied.

A HYNDLAND reader emails: "The way 2019 is going, I'm putting money on an alien invasion. Aliens: 'It's not an invasion, it's an intervention.'"

AND a reader heard a chap in his local post office, perusing the leaflet on what you can or cannot post internationally through the Royal Mail, declare: "Vodka, whisky, ammunition, cannabis, cocaine, fireworks, flares, flick knives and pepper spray. Where I come from that's got the makings of a right good party."

A QUICK mention of Boris Johnson. Writer Richard Fleeshman sees a similarity between the round-faced Boris and comedy actor Matt Lucas and wrote on social media: "Seriously though . . . has anyone ever actually seen Matt Lucas and Boris Johnson in the same room?" Actor Matt himself replied: "No. Because I would leave that room."

PRESIDENT Trump's faux pas of naming Prince Charles as the "Prince of Whales" on social media reminds us of The Diary's own affectionate stories about the Royal Family, including the reader who bought a lovely Prince Charles commemorative teapot and said the manufacturers had missed a trick by not adding the slogan, "It never reigns, but it pours."

CONGRATULATIONS to Tunnock's boss Boyd Tunnock on being knighted. Boyd is of course a Unionist in his politics, and when Alex Salmond was First Minister a reader pointed out to us that "Tunnock's Tea Cakes" was an anagram of "No tae Eck! Nats suck!"

DONALD Trump's visit to Britain reminds us of previous stories about Americans in The Diary including his predecessor Barack Obama claiming Scottish blood in his ancestry. "Would that be the Maryhill Baracks?" quipped a reader.

RUTHERGLEN Labour MP Gerard Killen wants all ATM machines to be free to use, although he doesn't explain how he would stop them simply being removed. Anyway, it reminds us of a reader who told us: "Has anyone else noticed the irony in being charged two pounds for simply taking money out of some ATMs while being warned to hide your PIN to avoid being robbed?"

CAN'T really avoid politics these days. Says Andrew Harrison: "Say what you like about Jeremy Corbyn, but he's built a mass movement from scratch, energised a party base, got it back to its true values and made it a power in the land. Unfortunately, that party is the Liberal Democrats."

LABOUR MSP Neil Findlay has announced he is going to stand down at the next election. Our favourite story about left-winger Neil was when he interrupted the SNP's Mike Russell in the parliament and Mike loftily declared, in the way that he does: "When Neil Findlay intervened, we were hearing an echo of Tommy Sheridan talking about class war. I knew, and was not a great supporter of, Tommy Sheridan. Mr Findlay is no Tommy Sheridan."

But Neil had the last laugh as he replied: "The wife will be pleased!"

TALKING about the Labour Party, former party spin doctor Alastair Campbell has announced that he has already been expelled from the party for voting for the Liberal Democrats at the European Elections just days earlier. Comedy actor Matt Lucas pointedly remarked on social media: "Dear Labour, that was quick. Yours, a Jew."

OUR story about a coach trip reminds former Ayrshire MP Brian Donohoe: "The story was told about the councillors on official business who had a 'good lunch' while away and on return the town clerk informed the provost that there was a £15 deficit on the bill for the lunch. The provost told the town clerk to leave it to him. He grabbed the mike on the bus they had hired and told his fellow councillors, 'I've just been informed by the clerk that we have a deficit of £15. I propose we give that to the driver. All in favour?'"

THE observation about new Scottish Secretary Alister Jack – never trust someone who can't spell their own name – sparked the contribution from George Smith in Clydebank: "Never trust anyone who does not use his first name – George Iain Duncan Smith, Alexander Boris de Pfeffel Johnson, and Gideon Oliver Osborne, who for some reason stuck George in front of it."

THE Queen was in Cumbernauld the other week as part of a mini tour of Scotland while on her way to Holyrood. As former councillor Gerard McElroy tells us: "As a Deputy Lieutenant of the county, I had a role to perform during the Queen's visit to Cumbernauld and thought I would dress appropriately. During the chat with the chap at the dress hire shop he enquired about the nature of the occasion. 'Well,' says I, 'I'm meeting the Queen coming off the Royal Train at Croy station.' 'Aye, very good, sir,' came the reply."

OUR mention of former Labour minister John Reid at a Labour conference reminds another Labour politician: "John was once being interviewed live by a female interviewer at conference when they were interrupted by what sounded like a Hoover. The bold John suggested they get the wee woman to stop. The interviewer took exception to that, asking John, 'How do you know it's a woman?' Quick as a flash, John answered, 'It's too fast to be a man.'"

WE see TV presenter Lorraine Kelly in the news for being a bit shirty with Tory leadership contender Esther McVey. Got to say Lorraine is always in a good mood when we bump into her. One year she flew up from London to Glasgow to present the Scottish Retail Awards with her dress over her arm, but the rest of her possessions were in a case that did not arrive with her at the airport. So, she just grabbed a taxi, walked into the Hilton with her dress, and asked the organisers if anyone had a pair of size six shoes as she didn't fancy presenting the awards in her trainers.

Dress shoes borrowed, off she went to do a splendid job on stage, and then told us afterwards: "My only worry was that my big pants that keep your tummy in were in my case so I had to do it without them."

TALKING of Brexit, Wetherspoons' boss Tim Martin, one of the few members of the business community in favour of leaving the EU, is touring the country explaining his views at specially arranged meetings in his pubs. He can be a smooth talker.

A Diary reader once met him in Glasgow's Esquire House, which had been bought by "Spoons" and he jokingly asked Tim why the pub's toilets, through five doors and down a flight of stairs, were so far from the bar. Instead of just shrugging him off, Tim went into an explanation that in the old days Glasgow bus conductors lived longer than drivers because they had to run up and down stairs all day.

"So really," he continued, "I'm doing the punters a favour by keeping them healthy."

A COLLEAGUE leans over my desk and informs me: "Donald J. Trump was asked what the middle initial in his name stands for. After a moment of presidential contemplation, he replied: 'Genius.'"

6

Fly Guys

With the pound tumbling against the euro and the dollar, it's surprising, but welcome, that folk can still find a laugh or two when they go on holiday.

AH, the holiday tales are beginning to drift in. A reader on holiday in Torremolinos in Spain heard a Scottish youth in a bar say to a young woman: "I bet I can talk you into taking off your T-shirt." The young woman dismissed his wager as extremely unlikely. At that the young lad added: "I've just seen a spider crawl inside it."

USING Airbnb to stay in someone's spare room is a great way to travel, but it can lead to misunderstandings. One woman traveller who had booked a room received the text message before she arrived stating: "I apologise in advance. But Kevin may try to sleep with you. Just keep your door shut." Her worried reply asking for an explanation received the message: "Kevin is my dog." A good example, she says, of why you shouldn't give your dog human names.

AUTHOR Rodney Lacroix revealed a post-holiday scenario that some folk might recognise: "Wife, 'Ugh, I gained three pounds during that vacation. What about you?' Me, looking at scales showing I actually lost a pound, 'I gained four.'"

YOUNG Scottish comedian Daniel Sloss once told of the fun he and his younger brother had when they went on holiday with their parents. Explained Daniel: "As soon as our dad started taking his belt off to go through the security scanner at the airport, we would look alarmed and shout out, 'No, Dad! I'm sorry!'"

BACK in the Highlands a reader was once dining in a hotel when an American diner complained to the waiter that his steak was tough and the vegetables undercooked. "Nothing like speaking your mind is there, sir?" said the waiter, before walking away.

OUR stories of folk abroad unexpectedly knowing about Scotland reminded Harry Clarke of being on a cruise where the young woman serving behind the bar, who was from the Philippines, on learning he was Scottish replied in a convincingly authentic accent: "Gonnae no dae that?" When he asked how she learned this gem she explained that The Krankies had been the onboard entertainment earlier that season.

HALFWAY through the Fair Fortnight, and a Glasgow reader tells us: "Was leaving the office last week and my boss shouted over: 'Don't think too much about your work when you're on holiday!' Do you think I went too far by shouting back: 'I don't even think about it when I'm here!'"

AS we are now well into the Glasgow Fair Fortnight, we pass on the observation by Dan Gibson: "Definitely getting old. My 19-year-old daughter is packing to go to Magaluf with friends tomorrow – well, she's supervising really, while my wife packs. She asks me, 'What do you think of these out-fits?' I ask her, 'Where's the rest of them?' Needless to say, it has been made clear my assistance is no longer needed."

AS we enter the second week of the Glasgow Fair, Gordon Casely recalls Fair Fridays of the past when drink was some-times taken. It still sticks in his mind that one Fair Friday in the 1970s he was the passenger in a Morris Marina birling along University Avenue in Glasgow's West End after a trip to the Halt Bar when they suddenly encountered two lads crossing the road carrying a significant length of rolled-up carpet. Not sure if the car could stop on time, the two lads merely lifted it higher above them and the car sped under the carpet.

"I never quite recovered from that, so hence my return soonest to home pastures in north-east Scotland," says Gordon.

THE holiday stories are beginning to find their way to The Diary, including the reader from Bearsden, on holiday with his family in San Francisco, who was buying tickets to catch the ferry across to the former prison island of Alcatraz. The American just ahead in the queue, who had a brood of children jumping up around him, asked the woman in the office for: "Two round trips, and three one way."

WE asked about your trips to France and Richard Hunter in Killearn says: "I clear up the dog poo – 'caca' in colloquial French – on the lawn of our French holiday house each week before my lovely gardener comes round to do his stuff. One week I said to him: 'J'ai fait le caca dans le jardin,' intending to say I'd cleared it for him as usual. We both split our sides when he asked me in French where in particular I'd done the caca."

TALES about visiting France, continued. Says Gavin Weir in Ayrshire: "On one of my first visits to Paris in the early 1980s, my wife, who had lived in France for some years, took charge while crossing roads as Parisians can be aggressive drivers. Leaving the Eiffel Tower to cross a busy road, she took my hand during a lull in traffic – only it was the hand of a tall, well-dressed African fellow this red-headed Scots woman grabbed to drag out onto the road. A big surprise for both of them."

NEARER home the Fair Weekend here in Glasgow reminds us of the elderly mum from Glasgow visiting her son in America during the Fair holiday and being asked on arrival at United States immigration: "Ma'am, do you have any meats, fruits or any other foodstuffs with you?"

"Aw, son," she replied sympathetically. "Ah huvny even a sweetie ah can gie ye."

THE vexed subject of giving up smoking prompts Cumbernauld reader Hugh Steele to recall an exchange in the works canteen one January, where one lass proudly announced she'd packed in the weed. Furthermore, with the savings made, she'd have enough by June or July to enjoy a package holiday abroad.

Recounts Hugh: "One of the other girls sighed: 'I wish I smoked so that I could give up and save all that money.'"

IT seems that more Scots have gone on cruises this summer. Among our favourite cruising stories in The Diary was the reader who told us that on an American cruise, when they went ashore in Mexico, they were handed a postcard of the liner which they could show to any taxi driver to take them back to the dock if their Spanish wasn't up to it and the driver didn't speak English. So he duly flashed the card at a taxi driver, but it didn't quite work. He drove them to the post office.

OK, we will mention the classic hot weather joke which is about the Glasgow couple who splashed out on an upmarket hotel in Spain where they found themselves lounging at the pool beside a history professor and his wife. The prof turned to the Glasgow chap and asked: "Read Marx?"

"Yes," he replied. "I think it's those wicker chairs."

MIDGES can be bad at this time of year, of course. A colleague once informed us: "I saw a sign in a shop 'Midge nets £10'. I didn't even know insects could play the Lottery."

FLYING back from Australia, a reader heard the passenger in front complain when the seat-back televisions were switched off just before landing. "My movie wasn't finished," he announced. "I'm sorry, sir," said the Australian attendant, "but we need to switch it off during our descent." "But I don't know how it ends," the passenger continued to wail. "They all lived happily ever after," announced the attendant as she carried on up the aisle.

DOWN memory lane, Diary readers once discussed when the weather was so hot that tar on the roads would melt. A reader recalled his dad owning a shop in Strathaven where one summer in the 1950s it was so hot his dad feared customers might drag melted tar over his new linoleum floor, so he covered it in newspapers. Ten minutes later his fed-up customers were walking about with sheets of newspapers stuck to their shoes like a bad Laurel and Hardy impersonation.

PARENTING can be difficult in the hot weather. A Knightswood reader once told us he bought his two young sons ice cream cones on an unusually sunny weekend. Not sure what they wanted, he returned with one vanilla ice cream and one chocolate, and asked the boys which one they wanted. Immediately one of the lads answered: "His!"

THE hot weather over the last few days reminds us of Diary stories in previous scorchers, such as the Glasgow girl at a job interview on a hot day who walked in and remarked: "S'awfy clammie!" The English chap conducting the interview replied: "Please take a seat, Sophie."

And the toper in the Glasgow pub who felt brave enough to tell his pals: "I was so hot in bed last night I had to cuddle up to the wife to get cold."

ONE of the hottest days in Britain yesterday. We liked the marketing savvy of the Waterstone's bookshop branch in Swansea which announced on social media: "Today is going to be HOT. Fortunately, we sell hand fans. They come in the form of sheets of paper glued or sewn together and bound in covers. We have many thousands of them in stock, and as an added bonus they have stories printed on them."

TALKING of mistakes Johnny Keats recalls: "My aunt wandered into an open-air restaurant in Greece and sat down. She had no Greek, and they had no English, so she pointed at what others were having and they brought her wine and food. Only when she tried to pay and they refused did she realise she'd just crashed someone's wedding party."

OUR story about the New York taxi driver being asked directions reminded Arthur Yaffy in Busby: "On holiday in Boston, we had arranged to visit the Museum of Fine Arts in the morning and in the afternoon go to Fenwick Park to watch a baseball game. On the map, these two places seemed to be quite close, so I thought that it would be convenient to park in the museum car park and later, walk to the baseball ground. When I parked at the museum, I asked the attendant, 'Can we walk to the ballpark from here?' He replied, 'Sir, you can walk to California from here.'"

AN EXPAT in Iowa sent us a joke from his local paper. "An American and a Scotsman are discussing ways to bring tourism to their countries. The American says, 'I'll build a theme park costing millions, employing thousands of people, which will bring people from around the world.' The Scotsman replies, 'I'm just gonna go down to the nearest loch and shout *What was that!* Should do the trick.'"

TIME to say Amen to our nun stories, but before we do, Barrie Crawford tells us: "I was on the Literary Pub Crawl in Dublin where a very funny but risqué piece involving nuns was read out and we all had a good laugh. After he had finished, our guide said that a group of American nuns had been on the tour and had reacted with stony silence.

"The group, though, repeated the tour the following night and when the guide asked them why they had returned when they appeared not to have enjoyed themselves, he was told, 'We wanted to laugh this time, so we've left the Mother Superior behind.'"

READER Larry Cheyne passes on: "Overheard on a cruise ship recently: 'The trouble with the Scots is that you can't understand what they say . . . and the trouble with the English is that you can.'"

OUR restaurant disaster stories remind Russell Smith in Kilbirnie: "Congratulating myself at being streetwise and choosing a Chinese restaurant patronised by the locals in Hong Kong, we were pleased to find large mugs of tea free of charge in addition to the modest prices, although admittedly the tea was pretty weak and barely lukewarm. When putting our trays away we found they were actually receptacles for depositing our used cutlery in."

A GLASGOW reader remembered going to Skye on holiday with his parents when he was a youngster. Arriving at a garage there, before self-service pumps, they could find no attendant. A man in his garden opposite shouted over: "Toot on yer horn." Our reader's dad replied: "I'm sorry, but I don't have the Gaelic."

AND a reader told us of his pal buying a house on Mull with the Gaelic name 'Tobar Dubh' – Black Well. He was so taken with the name that he spent days digging around the extensive garden to see if he could find the original well – but, despite his backbreaking efforts, he had no luck. He was later talking to the local shopkeeper, who told him about the previous occupants, and then added: "Before them there was an English couple, the Blackwells."

THIS year has seen the sad demise of Thomas Cook, the world's oldest travel firm. We prefer happier times when the firm released its favourite complaints from holidaymakers. They included:

"The brochure stated, 'No hairdressers at the accommodation.' We're trainee hairdressers – will we be OK staying there?"

"It took us nine hours to fly home from Jamaica to England. It only took the Americans three hours to get home."

"No one told us there would be fish in the sea. The children were startled."

"We bought 'Ray-Ban' sunglasses for five euros from a street trader, only to find out they were fake."

"I think it should be explained in the brochure that the local store does not sell proper biscuits like custard creams or ginger nuts."

A SECURITY scare on board an EasyJet flight to Glasgow yesterday reminded us of an excitable tabloid newspaper headlining "The Ugly Truth" when model Kate Moss caused a disturbance on an easyJet flight by swigging duty-free vodka from her cabin baggage on board and having a "sweary" altercation with a fellow passenger. A bemused reader told us: "Just sounds like your average EasyJet flight out of Glasgow."

And years ago, when entertainer Rory Bremner spoke

at the opening of the rebranded Dunblane Hydro after a multi-million-pound refurbishment, he said he had been at a function with EasyJet founder Stelios Haji-Ioannou. "Afterwards we shared a taxi," said Rory. "Stelios opened the door and said, 'After you.' He then charged me £10 for priority boarding."

A READER who returned from a holiday in Venice said he was in St Mark's Square when he heard a Scottish voice at a nearby table querying the rather large bill for two coffees. The waiter explained to him that there was a sizeable surcharge for the musicians playing in the background. "If I'd known,"

replied the Scotsman loudly, "that I was going to be paying for the music I'd have listened to it."

DUNOON, which is a bit run-down these days, wants to reinvent itself with a cable car to take you up the hill and zip slides to take the more energetic back down again. We remember a reader passing time in a Dunoon charity shop where he was admiring a miniature model of the famous Liberty Bell in Philadelphia, complete with its equally famous fissure. When he asked the lady in the shop how much it was, she said: "A pound." Then after investigating it further, she added: "Sorry, son, it's got a crack in it. I'll only charge you 50 pence."

ALAS, for those folk who will be returning unwanted Christmas presents. A reader in one store heard the elderly chap in the queue in front of her say the slippers he'd been given didn't fit, and he suspected there was something wrong with the size printed on the baffies. The assistant took the slippers to check they were undamaged, then asked the shopper: "Did you take the tissue out of the toes before trying them on?" Exit one embarrassed shopper.

THE airports can be busy at festive times of year and one reader recalled: "When my granddaughter was four, we went as a family group to Florida at Easter. At Glasgow Airport, we went through all the queues, check in, passport control, body scan, etc, which took over an hour. When we finally emerged into the departure lounge, my granddaughter asked, 'Are we in Florida now?'"

AH yes, the office Christmas parties. One Glasgow worker once told us: "At our office do we could bring our partners, so my wife met many of my co-workers for the first time. I can now tell how attractive the women in my office are by the number of times my wife told me an individual looked like a tramp."

WE also liked the story of the girl who arrived at her office Christmas party straight from a session in a tanning salon. Worried that the goggles had left a white ring around her eyes she asked her pal: "Do I look like a clown?"

    "Put it this way, Sophie," her pal replied, "Ah wouldnae be surprised if weans start asking ye fur balloons."

LOOKING back, one of our favourite New Year stories was the reader who told us about the chap in Dumfries who sent his sister in Canada a New Year telegram with the traditional Scottish greeting: "Lang May Your Lum Reek." She framed it on her wall as the chap at the Canadian end had typed it up as "Lang May Yer Bum Reek."

SO how's everyone getting ready for Christmas? We pass on the comment of one mother who declares: "All I want for Christmas is to sleep for nine hours straight, wake up to the sound of coffee brewing, and then ask questions like, 'What did WE get the kids for Christmas?' and 'How late were YOU up wrapping gifts last night?' Basically, I want to be my husband."

And one dad did tell us: "Merry Christmas to everyone, except the person who wrote the instructions on how to put this trampoline together."

GETTING a bit stressed at the time of year known as the festive season? As one reader puts it: "Drunk, Stupid or Old? is the game the driver in front of me doesn't know we're playing."

YES, it's that time of year when folk tell us Christmas yarns that unfortunately have featured in The Diary before. Such as the Ayrshire reader who told us how one member in the bar announced: "You've got to be careful on the roads before Christmas. A lot of men have had too much to drink at office parties – and their wives are driving instead."

Or the chap who announced in the pub: "The wife's been hinting she wants something black and lacy for Christmas. Do you think I should get her football boots?"

DID you enjoy Guy Fawkes Night? We always liked the description by a reader who told us: "Experience the anticlimax of a back garden firework display by setting fire to your wallet and throwing it over the shed."

A READER was once sitting beside a mother on a plane who breast-fed her baby during the flight. As they were coming in to land, the cheery steward checking seat belts, said to the mum: "She was hungry!"

"Not really," replied the mum. "It's just that my doctor said it would help alleviate the pressure in the baby's ears."

"Goodness," replied the steward. "And all these years I've been sucking sweets."

7

The Way They Tell Them

Scots do love a good night out, and never seem to be in awe of the stars they go to see. Here are some of their stories.

AMERICAN singer Norah Jones had one of her band whistling on one of her songs when she appeared at Glasgow's Armadillo, and she told the audience that she herself couldn't whistle. She explained: "I can't whistle blowing out the way, but I can do it a little bit drawing breath in the way. It's weird." To which a Glasgow voice shouted out: "It's called asthma, hen."

OUR story of the two theatregoers dressed as nuns reminded entertainer Andy Cameron: "In the 1980s I was filming sketches in Blythswood Square for a TV series with actress Teri Lally playing a nun. As we were waiting for lighting and sound to set up a Glesga guy comes round the corner having obviously enjoyed a wee libation at lunch time, looks at Teri, takes a pound note out of his pocket and hands it to her with the instruction, 'There y'are sister, put that in yer charity boax and God bless ye, hen.'"

SCOTTISH actor and comedian Craig Ferguson has written a memoir entitled *Riding the Elephant* and was being interviewed in American newspapers about his book and his life. His interviewer for the *Washington Post* said she missed his smile in his photograph on the book cover and unexpectedly asked: "Describe your smile."

Said Craig: "A miracle of American dentistry! Especially given that I grew up in Scotland in the 1970s."

WE asked for your Edinburgh Fringe stories and a reader reminds us of the old Malcolm Hardee Award for Comedy which was given out every year. He told us that one comedian appearing at The Counting House simply emailed the awards committee to nominate herself and then had printed on her posters: "Nominated for the Malcolm Hardee Comedy Award." Genius.

WE'RE just over three weeks to go until the Edinburgh Festival and are trying to think of our favourite gag from the Fringe. We can only come up with Ed Byrne's: "I have two boys, five and six. We're no good at naming things in our house."

AUSTRALIAN singer Nick Cave of Bad Seeds fame is on a tour of Britain entitled Conversations with Nick Cave where he invites inquiries from the audience about his life and career. Writer Fiona Sturges who was at one of the shows says: "Best question of the night, 'Hi, Nick. I live in your old flat in Hove. Do you know where the stopcock is?'"

WE do like the American acts that come to Glasgow. Country singer Otis Gibbs once told his Glasgow fans: "I had a really nice gig in Cardiff. Afterwards a guy walked up to me and said, 'I want you to know that your music saved my life.' I laughed and said, 'That's ridiculous,' but he said, 'It's true. I was in a coma for five months and the doctors weren't able to revive me. They'd given up hope. Then one day a nurse came in with a CD player and put in one of your CDs.

"'I immediately woke up, sat up on the edge of my bed, then walked across the room and turned off the CD player.'"

WE mentioned the presidential election in Ukraine. Entertainer David Walliams put the BBC story "Ukrainian comedian elected president" on social media and added the comment: "Mmm, this has given me an idea." His remark was topped, though, by a Gareth McCarthy, who replied: "You going to become a comedian?"

A GREAT film is *Wild Rose*, filmed in Glasgow and written by award-winning local writer Nicole Taylor. It's always good fun to spot the Glasgow locations, including the Silver-burn shopping centre.

As the British Film Institute revealed: "Striving for authenticity took the filmmaking team to such lengths they shot a scene where a despondent Rose-Lynn gets a job cleaning café tables at the city's Silverburn shopping centre. They couldn't get permission to film there, but true to Glasgow's rebellious spirit, shot the scene from a distance anyway, only for the café manager to stop Buckley cleaning with a terse, 'What are you doing?'"

A GLASGOW reader tells us a toper in his local was describing to fellow imbibers his trip to see the Rolling Stones in concert in Edinburgh this summer. He then felt the need to make a gag about it by adding: "I'm not saying Mick Jagger's getting on a bit, but he updated one of their singles and sang, 'Hey, You! Get Off Of My Lawn'."

TODAY'S piece of daftness comes from comedy writer Sanjeev Kohli who declares: "Singers Elaine Paige and Tina Turner have combined to write a book. I imagine it will be quite compelling."

DAN Edgar in Rothesay tells us: "You've mentioned before about singer Rod Stewart calling in at the Paisley pub the Wee Barrel on his way to Glasgow Airport. The proprietor, Willie Divertie, ran a no-nonsense establishment. On one of

Rod's many visits, he had the audacity to sign his autograph in lipstick on one of the ornate original wall mirrors. Mr Divertie was none too pleased, cleaned the offending autograph from the mirror and temporarily barred Rod from the pub."

GLASGOW stand-up and controversialist Frankie Boyle was discussing Scottish culture this week when he commented: "One thing Scottish culture has right is that you should put a knife in your sock if you're going to a wedding."

LOS Angeles-based singer-songwriter Sam Morrow was a recent guest on the award-winning Celtic Music Radio show

Mike Ritchie On Sunday. After discussing Sam's current album, and hearing him play three great songs on acoustic guitar, Mike asked him about the time he bumped into the American rhythm and blues and gospel singer, actress and civil rights activist, Mavis Staples, at her 80th birthday party.

Sam recalled the meeting well, revealing that Mavis said of his shoulder-length barnet: "I love your hair, honey."

Sam: "I love your hair, too."

Mavis: "I can take it off and let you wear it, if you like."

WE also liked the interview with performer Jack Tucker at the Fringe, which was carried in *Broadway World*, where he was asked: "How has the show been received so far?" Jack replied: "Incredible. Audiences absolutely love it. People get up on their feet, sometimes before the show's even done and walk out of the room to go and tell their friends about it! Sometimes this happens only 10 or 15 minutes into a show!"

AND Alan McKinney from Edinburgh asks: "How do you spot a tourist in Edinburgh?" and tells us: "At crossings – they are the only people waiting for the green man."

OVER in Edinburgh, the Festival Fringe has had its first weekend. The acts include a stage version of Radio 4's *Fags, Mags And Bags* comedy co-written by Sanjeev Kohli and Donald McLeary. After one show at the weekend Sanjeev was chatting with the cast outside the Udderbelly tent when a young family turns up, the mother clutching a pen and paper. "Are you Sanjeev Kohli?" she asked.

"Yes," he replied.

"Have you got a show on here?"

"Yes," Sanjeev confirms.

"Oh good," says the mum. "Can you go in and get us Basil Brush's autograph?"

AT the programme launch for Edinburgh Fringe venue the Gilded Balloon, comedian Fred MacAulay told the audience that, despite having lived in Glasgow for many years he, in fact, hailed from Perth. His opening gambit was: "I'll never be able to call myself 100% Glaswegian, though – I've retained the ability to mind my own business."

AS performers arrive in Edinburgh for the Fringe, comedian Lucy Porter has a look around town and remarks: "I see that the Edinburgh restaurant I've had a grudge against for 15 years (because they were rude to my parents) has now closed. Cross me at your peril!"

WHEN Tim Vine won a comedy award at the Edinburgh Fringe he declared: "I'm going to celebrate by going to Sooty's barbecue and having a sweepsteak."

SO, do you try to avoid folk handing out flyers at the Festival? An Irish comedian once told us: "My 12-year-old daughter is my secret flyering weapon. I have her wandering around outside my venue looking all sad and she goes up to strangers and says, 'Have you seen my daddy?' and people tell her, 'No, no. Sorry, love.' And she says, 'Well, you should,' and then she whips out a flyer and gives it to them."

ANOTHER Edinburgh tradition is performers reminiscing about how tough they had it. First up this year is writer Emma Kennedy, who recalled on social media: "My first Edinburgh I slept under a coffin. There was one toilet and one hand basin for 60 of us. I had two baths in six weeks. We had nothing to eat except cornflakes and pasta. We all got athlete's foot. I performed to an average of ten people and fell in love. It was brilliant."

Inevitably another performer replied: "At least you had cornflakes . . ."

TALKING of counting your blessings, we asked about unusual graces, and Eunan Coll in Coatbridge tells us: "At our all-male golf smoker a number of years ago, our captain recited the following grace – 'Oh sweet Saviour, Lord divine, who turned the water into wine. Please forgive this bunch of men, who are going to turn it back again.'"

TIME to clear the table on our unusual graces with David Miller sending us off by recalling one speaker at a dinner whose grace was: "Oh Lord, give us a good appetite, for much fine food is set before us. And Oh Lord, give us fortitude, for I have seen the toast list."

YOU can't beat a Glasgow audience. Mike Ritchie tells us: "The excellent singer-songwriter, Marseilles-based Terry Lee Hale, rounded off his gig at the Doublet in Glasgow the other evening with an unplugged, acoustic song. As he strummed the opening chords, he asked punters to his right: 'Can you hear me OK?' Back came the reply: 'Don't worry about it, it's fine. I've got your CD.'"

WE liked an interview with actor Kiefer Sutherland, who was showing his other talents as a singer and guitar player at Cottier's in Glasgow a few weeks ago, when he was asked why he was given the rather long name Kiefer William Frederick Dempsey George Rufus Sutherland.

He replied: "My mom and dad were really poor when I was born. The story from my dad is that he told people that if you feed me dinner tonight, I'll name my son after you."

SCOTS folk band the Tannahill Weavers were playing in Dayton, Ohio, supported on the bill by an American singer named Tom Scheidt, who immediately told them that he had played with inquisitive Scottish bands before, so before they asked, he could confirm that he did not, in fact, have a brother named Doug. Still, the Weavers were delighted to learn, after a few libations with Tom, that he had a cousin called Wayne.

ACTOR Arnold Schwarzenegger is returning for a role in the new Terminator film, *Terminator: Dark Fate,* which is coming out soon. Thinking about Arnold's longevity in the series, a reader phones to ask: "Will his catchphrase in the film now be, 'Ah, me back'?"

GLASGOW city centre was awash this weekend with noisy, brightly clad teenagers heading to the TRNSMT music festival at Glasgow Green. Not everyone was impressed by the fashions on show. As a lady called Dani exclaimed on social media:

"Absolute sick of the folk heading to TRNSMT – a sea of neon, Lycra and glitter. Looks like a unicorn shat everywhere."

SOME discussion among fans of the fantasy TV series *Game of Thrones* that the ending was not to their liking. As Danny comments, however: "Sorry if the TV series you have been watching for so long didn't finish the way you wanted. That happened to me with the 2015 General Election."

A READER phones us with the pertinent question: "Kyle, Paxman, Clarkson, Corbyn – is there anyone named Jeremy that doesn't gie ye the boak?"

NOW, who is willing to admit that they can agree with former *Strictly Come Dancing* contestant the Rev Richard Coles? The Rev colourfully declared yesterday: "How I know I'm fat: when I'm shaking, vigorously, an upturned Nando's Hot Sauce bottle my jowls flap like the sails of a caravelle rounding the Cape of Good Hope in a storm."

AH, the sheer daftness of stories that folk share on social media. Explained one couple: "We had gone to dinner and our hosts had cooked a recipe that they said they had got from the Hairy Bikers on TV. When they told us what we were about to eat we were saying, 'No way was chicken and kippers a thing, let alone a recipe from the Hairy Bikers.' We ended up tweeting the Hairy Bikers to ask them if they've ever done a chicken and kippers recipe – turns out it should have been chicken and capers."

END of an era as our old chum Jackie Bird leaves *Reporting Scotland*. I remember when Jackie officially opened the charity the Coach House Trust in the West End and told folk: "I was reading my son's workbook for school, in which he was encouraged to write about his family. So he had written: 'My mum puts on her best clothes, lots of make-up, and then goes out working at night.' I wondered what the teacher made of it."

And when Jackie was presenting a programme on new electronic aids for the blind, she highlighted a device that you held up to cloth and which told you its colour. She later remarked: "I couldn't resist putting it against my blonde locks – and then this voice intoned 'brown'!"

If you were wondering why there is a marvellous duck on the cover, we should mention that BBC4 ran a programme celebrating the old teatime telly magazine programme *Nation-wide*. A Glasgow-based former BBC employee worked on the show in the early 1980s when a film of a skateboarding duck was a big hit, so the hunt was on to find other unusual ducks.

"When a farmer in Norfolk phoned to say he had the oldest duck in Britain, a film crew rushed to his farm only," said our reader, "to career into the farmyard, drive straight over the aforementioned duck and flatten it."

THE children's charity Variety Scotland is holding a fundraising Ladies Luncheon at Mar Hall in May with Kate Robbins, singer, comedian, actor and voice-over artist entertaining the guests. It brings to mind of course Kate's story she told at the Edinburgh Fringe of being introduced to Princess Anne at a charity show. During the pre-show line-up, Anne chatted briefly with Kate and asked the question that royals have asked ordinary people for decades: "And what is it that you do for a living?"

"I'm an impressionist," said Kate.

"Do you have an exhibition on anywhere?" Princess Anne asked.

A FINAL adult film story as Ian McNair reminisces: "As teenagers we used to head to the New Bedford Cinema in the Gorbals on Friday nights for the X-rated House of Hammer horror movies double bill thinking we were pretty grown up. But stepping out into the Gorbals evening at the 10 p.m. pub chucking-out time was a whole lot scarier than anything we saw inside the cinema."

GREAT to see John Byrne's classic series *Tutti Frutti*, about the Majestics band, on the new BBC Scotland channel. We remember when National Theatre of Scotland director Vicky Featherstone adapted it for the theatre and she gushed in *The Stage* magazine: "To me, the Majestics are representative of a certain kind of working-class Scottish male, and the question is whether or not they're going to be able to reinvent themselves into a new kind of male in the 1980s."

When *The Stage* asked writer John Byrne what he thought of Vicky's adaptation he replied: "I was delighted and surprised – especially when she told me what it was really about. I had no idea."

THAT great American singer-songwriter Joan Baez was sounding as fresh as ever when she appeared at Glasgow's Concert Hall this week at the age of 78. As reader Barry Wilson from Paisley who was there tells us: "There was a standing ovation – from those of us who could stand, as we are all getting older. At the start of her second encore, a voice shouted out, 'You can stay all night!' Joan quickly replied, 'It's a while since I heard that proposition.'"

WHEN the Fopp record store on Glasgow's Byres Road faced possible closure, we recalled when former Fopp boss Peter Ellen was at a reception at Holyrood Palace where he was introduced to Prince Philip, who asked what he did. "I run music stores," said Peter, before a puzzled Philip barked: "Sheet music, is it?" Peter successfully fought the urge to reply: "No, for the most part it's pretty good."

The other Fopp store in Glasgow, in Union Street, once had a vending machine outside the front door to sell CDs round the clock. It didn't work out. The machine's mechanism was frequently clogged with photocopies of fivers, drawings of fivers, vouchers from other stores, and once a postcard from Ibiza.

GREAT film out just now about the career of Laurel and Hardy, entitled *Stan & Ollie*, which concentrates on their last tour of British theatres, including Glasgow. It reminds us of the tale told by the then-bellboy when the comedy duo stayed in Glasgow's Central Hotel. They asked to borrow a pencil from the bellboy and Oliver remarked that it was a small pencil. "Just like your tip," the lad told them, and the laughing duo upped their tip each from a shilling to half-a-crown.

NEWS reports said that Miles Richie, the model son of singer Lionel Richie, was arrested at London Heathrow Airport after becoming agitated when he was not allowed on a flight, and then claiming there was a bomb in his bag. More than one reader contacts us to ask: "Did you not wonder, when he was approached by the police, if he asked them, 'Hello, is it me you're looking for?'"

THE *Herald* reported that actor Gregor Fisher would play Rikki Fulton's morose minister character, The Rev I.M. Jolly, to mark the 40th anniversary of the BBC comedy sketch show *Scotch and Wry*.

Our old chum Tom Shields once asked Rikki how the Rev Jolly popped the question to his dragon-like wife Ephasia, and Rikki solemnly replied: "It was a misunderstanding, actually. They had gone for a fish tea at the Ritz Fish and Chicken Bar and afterwards, as she helped him into his taxi, he mumbled, 'I'll give you a ring sometime.' The magistrate ruled that a definite proposal had been made."

AUTHOR Barbra Paskin has just published a book on the late entertainer Dudley Moore, entitled *Dear Dudley*, which includes copies of the many letters that celebrities sent him to cheer him up on his 64th birthday when he was ill. We liked the one from Des O'Connor who reminded Dudley in his letter: "I remember you telling me what your mum said when she saw you nude in the film *10*. 'Oh Dud, I saw all your bits and pieces and I haven't seen those since you were a baby . . . and you haven't changed a bit.' I'm still getting laughs in concerts with that story."

A HILLHEAD reader sees in the *Radio Times* that *Strictly Come Dancing* judge Bruno Tonioli confessed that in the 14 years he has been a judge he has never actually watched a single episode of *Strictly*. "Didn't realise we had so much in common," says our reader.

SCOTS comedian Karen Dunbar is returning to the King's Theatre in Glasgow next summer for a two-week run of the musical comedy *Calendar Girls*. We remember when Karen appeared at the King's in her first panto, *Sleeping Beauty*, alongside the late great Gerard Kelly. She told a press conference that Gerard had advised her just to be herself on stage and not attempt to be Meryl Streep. The next question was from a reporter who asked: "What will you bring to the role?"

"Sliced sausage," replied Karen.

ACTOR Alan Cumming is to receive an outstanding contribution to film and television award at the Scottish Baftas next month. Older readers will recall that Alan first made his name with fellow actor Forbes Masson with their comedy stage show *Victor and Barry* which was about two Kelvinside thespians.

A young reporter on the *Scotsman* gave the show such a

bad review that they incorporated the reporter into a version of Dean Friedman's song 'Lucky Stars' with the line "We can thank you, Andrew Marr, that you're not as smart as you'd like to think you are." We wonder whatever happened to that young reporter?

CONGRATULATIONS to Shereen Nanjiani being made an MBE for services to broadcasting. We always liked her explanation of how she moved from being a reporter at STV to presenting the main nightly news programme. Our old chum David Scott was head of news at the time, and as Shereen once recalled: "David, a very gruff news boss, called me in and said, 'Right, you're reading the news tonight.' I was aghast and immediately said I couldn't possibly do it. 'I've had no training.' He said, 'Don't worry, if you f**k it up you won't be doing it again.'"

OUR tales of awkward introductions remind former *Still Game* actor Jimmy Martin: "I was introduced to a woman at Partick Cross by a mutual friend who said, 'This is Jimmy, he works in television.' 'I wish tae God you'd come up and look at mine,' she replied. 'I don't know what's wrong with it.'"

TV quiz champion Paul Sinha, who appears on the show *The Chase*, was at Glasgow's Stand Comedy Club as he also does stand-up comedy. When he arrived in Glasgow, Paul explained: "My cab driver said, 'You look a bit like a slimmer version of the guy off *The Chase.'* Now that's how you earn a tip."

THE Glasgow Film Festival ended with one of the stand-outs being the French film *Le Monde est à toi* (*The World Is Yours*), a rollicking crime caper with English actor Sam Spruell playing a foul-mouthed Glasgow drug dealer in Benidorm.

When asked how he prepared for the role he explained: "I had just finished a play in London, but I spent a day wandering around Benidorm. It's awash with drink and lawless. By the end of the day I reckoned I'd nailed it."

8
Being Childish

"Where would be without our children?"

"On a beach in the Bahamas with thousands of pounds in the bank," the churlish would respond.

But we do love our children, really, and Diary readers are always keen to pass on the funny gems from their children.

A READER declares: "My grandchildren love hearing stories of when I was growing up in the 1960s – roller skates you had to tie on to your shoes, disappearing all day without your folks worrying, sweets from the penny tray. So, I told them next time I'm looking after them I'll treat them to a 1960s experience. They don't know I'll go to the pub for a pint and leave them sitting outside with an Irn Bru and a packet of crisps."

WE like parents' confessions about bringing up their children, and we detect just a hint of bitterness as a female reader declares: "My kids ask me why I wear so much black. I told them it's because I'm in mourning for the body I used to have before they came along."

YES, Glasgow was awash with neon-clad youngsters enjoying the TRNSMT music festival at Glasgow Green. Older readers who used to go to festivals might recognise the memories of one young girl, Laurie, who put on social media: "To be honest, isn't the whole point of TRNSMT getting so s**t-faced you don't remember any of the acts, and have to leave before the headliner comes on? If not, I don't think Jane and I did it right."

And another young girl commented: "The highlight of my TRNSMT was walking into a pole on the way home."

WE mention Chic Murray a lot, and a Falkirk reader makes an interesting point: "One of my favourite jokes of his was when he said he had fallen and was lying in the street when an old woman came up and asked, 'Have you fell, son?' He answered, 'Naw, I'm just trying to break a bar of toffee in my back pocket.' "Would today's youngsters ever buy a bar of toffee, far less know how hard it was to break one?"

THAT great day out, the Royal Highland Show, is on just now at Ingliston. You can't beat it for being able to buy a two-pound jar of honey or a combine harvester for a quarter of a million quid on the same site while strolling past highland cattle having their hair blown dry before going in the ring.

Our favourite Highland Show story was the year there was a Tannoy announcement for everyone to be on a lookout for a missing schoolboy. It turned out that he got his face camouflaged at the Army stand, then felt he had to hide from his teachers until they finally winkled him out.

EYES down for our final gawky grace story as Robin Mather in Musselburgh tells us: "Years ago, my parents were elders of the Church of Scotland which meant we had several ministers coming to our home to visit. On one occasion, as we sat down to our evening meal, our guest asked if he could say grace. Seeing the look of concern on my face, he said, 'Don't worry, son, this won't take long.' He went way up in my estimation as he uttered, 'Ta, Pa.'"

YES, it was Father's Day yesterday, and of course folk were on social media detailing how great their fathers are and expressing how much a difference their fathers make to their lives. But we prefer the honesty of one Scottish father who merely wrote: "Only had to text my girls four times to get them to bring me a coffee in bed. Happy Father's Day."

UP in the Western Isles reader John Mulholland tells us about a family passing by the mosque in Stornoway on Friday, and their son, who was about six, on seeing many pairs of shoes outside, asked what was in the building. The mother explained it was a bit like a church, a place where Muslim people went to pray to God. "Can we go to that church, Mummy?" asked the boy excitedly. "I think it's got a soft-play area!"

A READER swears to us that he bumped into an old pal at the Newton Mearns shopping centre yesterday who told him: "We're looking after our grandson today. His electronic drum kit has stopped working so I've come down with him to get batteries. Told him it takes quadruple-A batteries, but the shops don't seem to have any."

A PIECE of whimsy from a reader who emails: "Sibling relationships are strange; like I'd give my sister a kidney, but I wouldn't let her wear my clothes."

I WAS shocked when I read in the *Evening Times* that the factors of a Bishopbriggs housing estate wanted to ban children from playing hopscotch as the chalk disfigured the pavement – I mean, when did it become hopscotch and not the perfectly acceptable Scottish word peever?

We are reminded of a classic Bud Neill cartoon of a typical Neillian lady with her small son over her knee raising clouds of dust from his backside as she declares: "I'll teach you tae play peever wi' yer maw's tap set."

A PIECE of whimsy from a West End reader who tells us: "I remember when I was a child my dad said, 'I'll give you something to cry about.' He didn't hit me. What he meant was destroying the housing market, melting the ice caps, cutting down the rainforests and polluting the oceans with plastic."

FOLK are discussing bringing up kids after Prince William jokes about Prince Harry joining the sleep deprivation club. As one mother explained: "A friend wanted to know what it's like to be a mother, so I battered down her bathroom door while she was taking a shower so I could tell her that I'm thinking about changing the name of one of my stuffed animals."

And a father adds: "Probability tells you that a toddler has a 50-50 chance of putting their shoes on the correct feet. Parenting tells you otherwise."

OVER in America, the *New York Post* has reported that pregnant Royal bride Meghan Markle "plans to take three months of maternity leave".

"From what?" asked a reader.

WE mention the difficulties of bringing up young children, and a grandmother tells us: "My three-year-old grandson threw a crying fit when he couldn't wear his favourite trousers as they no longer fitted him. His mother merely told him, 'I know how you feel son.'"

SOME of you might look back to your youth and identify with the 20-year-old girl, Lizzie, who admitted on social media this week: "Told my dad I ran out of alcohol and didn't have any money to buy any for the weekend . . . so he gave me the huge bottle of vodka from the cupboard that I stole and replaced with water when I was 16. Life really does come back to bite you on the backside."

THE *Herald* reported the Wee Free minister who declared the Scottish Government's smacking ban was an attack on the authority of God. It reminds us of the reader who told us she was in Glasgow's Buchanan Street where a child was screeching to his mother that he wanted to go to McDonald's. Eventually, in sheer exasperation, she tugged him along and shouted: "It'll be SmackDonald's you'll get if ye don't shut up."

PARENTING, continued. Says a Hyndland reader: "My daughter offered me a bit of her chocolate bar. I was surprised as she's not much of a sharer. Just as I was chewing away her brother came storming in demanding to know where his chocolate bar was, and giving me a hurtful look when he saw me chewing. His sister will go far."

WE asked for your stories of strict parents and Robert Gardner recalled: "I went to the Scout Jamboree in Greece when I was 16, camping on the Marathon Plains. I sent a long, detailed postcard home telling my parents what was happening. When I arrived back, I found my mother had marked the postcard out of 10, giving me a very low score and then left it on the mantelpiece. From that day on, any cards sent home only had one word. 'Fine' in the centre of the writing space."

RAISING children, continued. A reader passes on a comment from a female friend: "I told my children that occasionally I need some 'Me time', which is when they should leave me alone. I didn't realise they would make it happen when the bins need taken out, when the table needs set, and when the shopping has to be brought in from the car."

THE things children say. Boyd Houston in Dollar tells us: "The only conservatory key had gone missing. I challenged our eight-year-old granddaughter, the undoubted suspect. She denied any involvement but did say that she knew that another little girl, who was a bit of a minx, had hidden the key in a black bag in the loft! Sure enough, the key was found."

A BEARSDEN reader gets in touch to tell us: "I took my grandson to a shopping centre toilet and when he was drying his hands in one of their powerful hand-driers I was telling him that in my day the driers were so weak that no matter how long you used them you still left with your hands wet. It was only later I remembered my grandfather telling me about his best friend at school dying of polio so yes, perhaps we didn't have it so hard growing up after all."

ROBERT C. Kelly knows the first rule of showbiz: optimism. The Glasgow-based theatre producer takes this maxim into his private life, too. "Bad news," he grumbles on social media. "In the past week I have had one trip to the dentist for two extractions and now on second trip to the orthodontist since Thursday."

However, there's an upside to Robert's tale of woe: "Good news," he adds. "It's for the kids, so I haven't felt a thing!"

WHO can agree with Felicity who declares: "I feel sorry for Netflix-era kids. They will never know the high stakes adrenaline of running to the bathroom/fridge/bedroom in a single ad break, with the beckoning call of a sibling screaming 'It's on!' to send you hurdling over furniture to get back in time."

SOME parents can be a tad competitive, and brag a bit on social media. As Valerie put it: "A friend wrote a Facebook tribute for her son's second birthday where she called him 'an explorer' and I'm like, 'Calm down, Trisha, all toddlers love sticking their hands in toilets. Greyson is no exception.'"

A JORDANHILL reader tells us that her upset-looking young daughter rushed up to tell her: "Just for fun I barked at our dog, Mummy, and he looked really surprised. I'm worried that maybe I said something really nasty to him in doggy language."

YES, that Amazon Echo Dot with its ever-available Alexa to answer your questions is changing our lives. John Dunlop tells us: "My three-year-old grandson, having just been told off, announces: 'Alexa, give Mummy a row!'"

READER Lewis Brown recalls his young son's confusion watching a football match on the telly. "The commentator keeps talking about the skipper," said the confused youngster. "Which player's he?" Dad explained that skipper was another name for the captain.

"Oh," came the disappointed reply. "I thought maybe it was someone good at skipping round the pitch."

9

Saved by the Bell

And before you know it, your youngsters are off to school. Parents and teachers shared their favourite stories with us.

WE remember one Glasgow reader who realised his son, going into Primary 6, was getting older when he stopped him at the door and said he wanted to take his picture, as he had done in previous years. But this time his son just brushed past him, held up his hand and said: "Not a good time."

OUR children at school stories reminded Michael Gartlan: "A teacher I know was telling her primary class about the 100th anniversary of the end of the First World War in November 2018 and how we should remember the sacrifice of all the men and women who suffered in that conflict. One of her six-year-olds announced that her granddad had won a medal in that war. Next day the youngster proudly showed the medal. Printed on it was 'Congratulations. One year sober'."

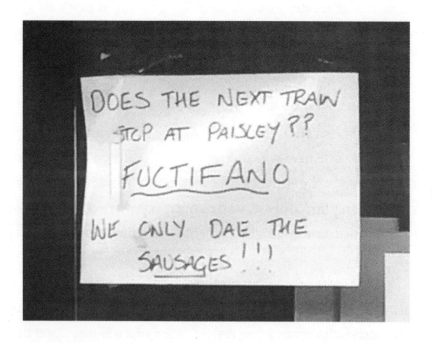

AND talking about schools, Brian Collie recalls: "We had two teachers at secondary school – Mr Murphy, who took us boys for athletics, but I think he was a science teacher, and Miss Barr, girls' gym teacher. They got married – probably why the science teacher hung around the gym, now I think of it – and had a baby . . . christened by the pupils as 'The Murphy Barr Kid'."

THE *Herald* news story about private schools in Edinburgh being under financial pressure reminds us of a reader who was at Edinburgh Airport to check in for a flight and heard the family in front of him being asked for identification even though it was only a domestic flight to London.

As the parents desperately scrabbled about in pockets and bags, their lad, wearing the uniform of a local private school, showed his future leadership qualities by stepping forward and declaring: "My name is sewn into the back of my jumper."

WE'VE all been there I suspect. A Glasgow primary teacher tells us she had just seen the last of the children into school after the bell had gone when a harassed mother hurried over with her daughter and announced: "Sorry we're late. Today's the day Ava announced she could zip up her jacket by herself."

A NEWS story about mining reminds us of the Glasgow schoolteacher who confronted a pupil who had decided she was a goth, complete with too much make-up as far as the teacher was concerned. "My grandfather used to come up from the coal mine looking like that," he told her, but was put off his stride when she replied: "What? Did he wear mascara, too?"

SCOTTISH company TeeJay Publishers provides most schools in Scotland with their maths textbooks. Tom Strang at TeeJay received a phone call from a boy saying he was having trouble with a question in one of their textbooks. Tom tells us: "I looked out the question in the book and told the boy it was too complicated to explain over the phone and he should ask his teacher instead. 'Ah cannae, mister,' the boy whispered very quietly. 'A'm sittin a test.' Needless to say, he got short shrift."

ONE pugnacious pupil, we recall, didn't stand a prayer of passing religious education. His exasperated teacher once ordered him to stand up and tell the class the Ten Commandments. The pupil hesitated, so, to encourage him, the teacher said: "In any order you like."

The pupil finally stammered: "Eight, six, ten, one, four, nine, five, two, seven, three."

WE mentioned poet Hugh McMillan, author of *The Conversation of Sheep*, failing at a Young Famers' quiz night because of his then-lack of knowledge of sheep.

A reader in Milngavie tells us of a new teacher in Lochmaben, Dumfriesshire, who attempted to draw a sheep on the blackboard for her class of seven-year-olds. "Well, boys and girls, this is an easy one – what do you think that is?" She was shocked that no one answered, so she cajoled one of them: "Come on now, Angus, what is it?" Eventually Angus replied: "Well, miss, um, is it a cross between a Cheviot and a Blackface?"

OUR stories of presents for teachers reminds Bob Mathieson: "Some years ago, when my wife was teaching in a school in Airdrie, a pupil regularly brought in some doughnuts for her favourite teacher. When the teacher complained that this was too much, the wee lassie said it was OK, because her Mammy worked in Dalziel's bakery and smuggled them out in her knickers. Needless to say, the staffroom saw a severe shortage of doughnuts for a long time."

WE always like our readers' schoolchildren stories. Says Ada McDonald: "A favourite family story is when one of the family, aged about six, came home from school very upset, and announced she was too frightened to go back. The reason was that she was to have a new teacher who was absolutely terrifying, so much so that she was called MacTiger. So, the next day, mother went to school to clarify the situation, and met the 'terrifying' new member of staff – a Miss MacTaggart, a charming lady. After a somewhat wary return to school, normal service was resumed."

PUPILS can reveal quite a bit about their home life, and one wee boy excitedly told the class that when they were away for their summer holidays their house had been broken into. "That's terrible," soothed the teacher. "Did they know who did it?"

"My dad said it was bastards," replied the little one.

WE return to the topic of trying to talk proper as a retired teacher in Bishopbriggs recalls in his teaching days that they were pushing their charges to use proper English when talking to a teacher. He tells us: "A teacher coming out of the staffroom, which lacked a window, asked a boy outside what the weather was like. He thought for a moment, and replied, 'Whole stones!'"

OUR tales of meeting your children's teachers remind Duncan McIntyre: "We went to the school parents' night, and while we were waiting our turn, we noticed several people looking at the children's work, then looking at us rather strangely. When our turn came, we found that our daughter had written, 'My worst moment was when I woke up and found a strange man in mummy's bedroom.' Nowhere had she said that mummy had appendicitis and that the man was the doctor."

EAST Renfrewshire has been ranked the happiest place to live in Scotland in a new analysis by Royal Mail based on markers including life expectancy, crime levels and earnings. It reminds us of a story in the *Times Educational Supplement* which recorded a schools' inspector visiting an East Ren school and asking the little tots for an example of something that normally came in a dozen. It was the first time he got the answer: "Oysters."

TALKING of posh, our cockroach in the soup story reminded Alasdair Sinclair: "When I was a prefect at Oban

High in the 1950s a boy complained that he could not eat his mince as there was a maggot in it. I took the offending plateful to the teacher in charge that day. He peered at it, called for silence and said, 'It has been brought to my notice that someone has found a maggot in his mince. When I was in the army, we were lucky to get mince in our maggots.' Then he sat down and continued to eat his lunch."

WITH Christmas hurtling towards us, we mentioned tales of children giving their teachers presents. As reader Willie Downs passes on: "There was the wee lad who gave a small but lovely bunch of flowers to his teacher, saying, 'I'd a got you mair, miss – but the wumman chapped the windae.'"

NOSTALGIA alert! We are well down memory lane as Ada McDonald tells us, following our stories about pupils giving gifts to teachers: "My aunt's friend was a primary teacher in Glasgow's Tradeston area in the 1940s. Money was in short supply, but the children used to bring her small gifts – an apple, a scone or a sweet were popular gifts. One wee boy could not quite rise to that standard but he was determined to bring something. He arrived one day with something soggy in a paper bag. 'What's this you've brought me, Billy?' 'Please, miss, it's the peas oot o' ma soup.'"

RETIRED teacher Margaret Thomson passes on: "Years ago I was taking my Primary 2 class in after playtime. I noticed that wee Jim was still carrying his play-piece, a banana. I asked why he hadn't eaten it, and he said, 'Please, miss, I couldn't get its trousers down.'"

SOME 400 children swarmed Milngavie Town Hall the other day for the local Primary Schools Scottish Dance Festival, held by the Royal Scottish Country Dance Society, which is celebrating its 95th anniversary. Patrick Murray, one of the dance instructors, tells us: "I turned up at a school for the final rehearsal in full Highland dress. Taking out my sgian-dubh, and emphasising that you shouldn't take knives to school, and ignoring requests to pass it around, I went on to say the Gurkha Regiment had a ceremonial knife called the Kukri which was much larger, and as a matter of honour they had to draw blood – just a small thumb prick from someone would suffice – before putting it back.

"I then went on to pass around my sporran, and then it was back to the dance. But just then a wee girl nervously put her hand up. 'Mr Murray, when are you going to start taking blood?'"

10

Off to Yoonie

And the laughs don't end when your children leave school. There is also humour in the university years.

A READER having a pint in London was watching the news on the telly when the newsreader announced that Glasgow University had been evacuated after a suspicious package had been found. "What? A salad?" said a toper further up the bar.

ON the topic of TV licences, Neil Shepherd in Orkney tells us: "While a student in Aberdeen halls, a friend received a warning phone call from the downstairs neighbour that the inspector was on his way up. The TV was quickly hidden in a cupboard and the inspector was shown around a room where all the furniture was facing an empty table in the corner with a TV-shaped square surrounded by dust. He nodded then moved onto the next flat."

GOOD to see the students at the University of West of Scotland campaigning to have the fee you have to pay to graduate being dropped. When you add that on to the cost of a gown hire and official pictures it can cost a right few quid. We recall the reader who swore to us that he attended a graduation ceremony in Glasgow where he witnessed a sobbing grandmother hug her graduating grandson and tell him: "Your parents would have been so proud seeing you up on that stage today." After giving him another squeeze, she added: "It's a shame they couldn't be bothered to come."

OUR tales of students reminded Ronnie McLean: "I remember reading a report of a court case back in the 1960s in your sister paper, the *Evening Times*. A witness was describing the odd behaviour of the accused and said, 'I thought he was either drunk or a student.'"

WE brought back memories with our story about the students' charity day in Glasgow, and Andy Cameron recalls: "As a conductor on a number 14 bus heading for St Enoch Square my bus was invaded by a group dressed as a gorilla, a dental nurse and a rather large alien who said they were there to extract your cash. As they disembarked a grumpy Glesga wummin chastised a priest who had got on at Ellington Toll with, 'Ur you just gonny sit therr and let them dae aw the collecting? Get up aff yer arse and gie them a haun!'"

धुम्रपान निषेध

LUNGS AT WORK PL. DON'T SMOKE

MANY of the halls of residence for Glasgow University are up in Maryhill. A student who was staying there once told us he was walking along Maryhill Road when a wizened-looking chap asked him if he could spare a fag. "I don't smoke," replied the student. "So, you're not fae Maryhill then?" the chap opined.

WE heard about a Milngavie teenager who moved to a student flat in Glasgow and asked his mum how to cook a meal as he had a new girlfriend coming round for dinner. Afterwards his mum phoned to ask how the meal went, and he told her: "Not so great. She wanted to wash the dishes." "What's wrong with that?" asked his mum. "It was before I'd served the food," he explained.

SO unfair when people look down on students who attend further education colleges instead of university. As one chap declared on social media the other day: "I went to uni in Edinburgh at the start of the 1980s. In those days you could sign on during the holidays, so the council set up special sign-on centres for students – mine was at Tollcross. The lad in front goes up to the wifie and she says, 'I've got a form for you to fill in, which college do you go to?'

"'Stevenson', the lad replies.

"'Hang on a tick, I've got something for you to fill in the form with', and she reaches in her desk and pulls out a crayon.'"

RAISING teenagers, continued. Many will probably have been in the position of Simon Holland, who commented: "One side of our sink has a garbage disposal. The other side is where my daughter just dumped a full bowl of cereal."

ANYONE with teenage children will know that ID cards from folk over 21 are constantly borrowed in order to get into clubs. One bouncer tells us: "Someone accidentally handed me his real ID instead of his fake. I said: 'This says you're 19,' and he replied: 'That's my old one, here's my real ID,' and he handed me an entirely different person's ID as if his name and birthday had magically changed."

WONDER how many people would agree with actress Amanda Abbington, who declared: "Cleaning out my son's bedroom. If I was filming it, it would be the groundbreaking follow-up to the hit series *Chernobyl*. Only with more cata-strophic radiation and devastating results."

IT was also the anniversary of William Shakespeare's birth-day this week. As one mother declared: "Shakespeare is widely considered the world's greatest dramatist. But only by people who haven't met my daughters when their hair or make-up isn't going right."

OUR mention of students arriving home for Easter reminds a reader: "In my student flat we were so lazy that no one wanted to do the washing-up. It dawned on us how bad it was that we found ourselves drinking whisky out of eggcups as every other cup and tumbler needed washed."

WE pass on the observation from freelance journalist Dayna McAlpine in Edinburgh who spent a few years working in London: "My pals think living in Scotland is all beautiful rolling hills and friendly patter when in reality it's a junkie shouting, 'Ye going' for a s***e, hen?' at me because I'm carry-ing a 16-roll pack of toilet paper."

WE mentioned La Bonne Auberge in Glasgow ordering more than 80 fancy gin glasses with their name and logo printed on them, only to be left with just 16 of them after Christmas. We didn't expect one reader to tell us: "Must go in tomorrow and bag one of the last 16."

Anyway, on the question of glass appropriation, Lesley Wilson tells us: "I was a student at Dunfermline College of PE in Cramond, Edinburgh, an all-female establishment a bit like St Trinian's. Our local was the Cramond Inn which we visited with appropriate student enthusiasm.

"College uniform included a dark cloak – perfect for hiding pints for the thirsty walk back to the residences. At the end of each term, the inn left a box at the entrance to the residences with a note threatening a ban next term if we didn't return the glasses we'd 'borrowed'. It was filled to overflowing every time."

11

A Senior Moment

Confessions are good for the soul, and a lot of *Herald* readers like to confess their senior moments when they have reached the age of qualifying for a cheap haircut at the barber's.

READER Mary Duncan told us: "My bowling club friend Margaret was absolutely delighted to get her bus pass. First time using it, not knowing you're supposed to state your destination, she proudly put it on the scanner and waited expectantly.

Driver: 'Where are you going?'

Margaret: 'I'm going to the hairdresser's.'

Driver: 'Yes, but where are you going?'

Margaret: 'Well, I'm going to meet my mum and then I'm going to get my hair cut and . . .'

The driver was struggling to be heard above the laughter

of the other passengers as he once again asked where she was going."

The cooking of roast dinners, bacon, egg or sausage sandwiches, is prohibited whilst in the lock

Please pass all such items to lockstaff for safe disposal

RETIRED doctor John Hay in the Western Isles tells us he was perturbed when listening to the BBC news on the radio, reporting on the out-of-control wildfires in Europe during the current continental heatwave, to hear that "musicians might blow up". He was trying to work out how that could possibly happen until he heard on a later broadcast that it was in fact ammunition on an army base threatened by the conflagration in Germany, and he has vowed to have his hearing tested.

WE know a few of you will identify with this as a Whitecraigs reader sends us a new take on a very old joke. He tells us:

"The chicken crossed the road for the same reason everyone else does – to avoid running into someone it knew."

GROWING old, continued. Says a Woodside reader: "Childhood injuries: Fell off my bike, fell out of a tree, twisted my ankle. Adult injuries: Slept wrong, sat down too long, sneezed too hard."

WHO can agree with Hannah Williams who remarked on social media: "I appreciate this marks the start of my descent into a lonely death, surrounded by hundreds of cats, but I have now taken to picking up rubbish while walking around my neighbourhood . . ."?

A friend of Hannah's replied: "Keep us informed when

you reach stage two of shouting at random people in the park about minor infringements of council by-laws."

SAYS a Pollokshaws reader: "Surely I'm not the only person who religiously asks the wife on a Friday night what the plans are for the weekend and she tells me. Then on Saturday morning first thing I ask, 'What are we doing this weekend?'"

QUERY of the day: "Does the Queen ever study a freshly minted five pence piece?" muses Tom Ferguson from Shettleston. "Then say to herself: 'Ooft, I've let myself go!'"

THINGS that only happen in the summer. We pass on the concern of young Kim from Brechin on social media, who told her pals: "Looked out the window and the wee wifie next door was lying on the ground. Thought she'd fallen, and near ran out to help her till I realised she was just weeding her garden."

GROWING old, continued. Says Tim: "Why is it I can somehow remember the lyrics of a song from the 1970s that I've probably not heard since then, yet I have to look at a boarding pass at least 20 times in quick succession to simply remember what seat I'm in?"

SAYS a Clarkston reader: "I noticed that a neighbour had a big party at the weekend. Years ago, I would have taken the huff at not being invited, but now I realise I'm at the age where I was just relieved I wasn't."

A SOUTH side reader tells us: "I was asked my age the other day in a shop and my mind suddenly went blank. So, I thought I would quickly subtract the year of my birth from this year, but then for a moment I couldn't remember what year it is just now. So I just guessed how old I was."

GROWING old, continued. Says a Newton Mearns reader: "Now when I run into an old friend I haven't seen for a while I have to stop myself from saying the first thing that comes into my head, which is usually, 'I thought you were deid.'"

ADMITS Craig Deeley: "My middle-aged version of an adrenaline-fuelled race against the clock is getting all four tyres checked and pumped up before the timer stops."

GROWING old, continued. A Renfrewshire reader tells us: "When I was in my twenties someone described me as 'wild and untamed'. Now I reserve that description for my eyebrows."

CONFESSES David Donaldson: "A good indication that your memory is not what it used to be is when you buy a nice book in the charity shop as a surprise for your wife and she gently points out that it bears a remarkable resemblance to the one you donated a few weeks back."

MUSES George Crawford in West Kilbride: "I suspect that a sign of getting old is when you find yourself reminiscing about a time when the tomato sauce bottles were the right way up."

TALKING of growing old, a reader tells us her friend, married to a Scotsman, is German, and still struggles with British idioms. She was asked how she was coping with her husband who had recently retired being at home, and she replied that she was fed up with him being between her legs all the time.

CAN imagine a few folk will sympathise with writer and stand-up David Baddiel who revealed: "Sometimes when my memory fails me now with names, I just decide to say the name that my brain is suggesting to me as its best attempt, out loud. The other day while trying to tell my wife something about artist Grayson Perry I said, 'Oh you know . . . Bunty Chudley."

SAYS Bob Jamieson: "Driving home from golf with a friend, we were discussing how many things we forgot each day. He responded by telling me that he had a system. Every night before he went to bed, he remembered three things that he would need next day. Keys, phone and . . . he couldn't remember the third.

"Two hours later I received a text, which simply said, *Wallet*."

A GLASGOW reader asks: "Why is it that when you are at a social gathering at a friend's, and someone suggests playing a game, and you say you don't know how to play it, you are suddenly confronted by seven people who all yell different rules at you all at once?"

GROWING old, some further thoughts. Says Barry Harper: "Sadly the Monopoly board game made me believe that as an adult there would be a lot more bank errors in my favour than has actually turned out."

GROWING old, continued. A reader gets in touch to tell us: "As you get older, you begin to miss the little things. Like the next stair."

And reader Patricia Allison says: "My grand-daughter aged eight laid out a card memory game on the carpet and then announced, 'Granny, I'm going for a pee now, so you make a start at getting down on to the floor.' A bit harsh, I thought. Observant though!"

12

It's the Law

Even being stopped by the police can bring out a flash of humour in our fellow Scots.

OUR stories about the police reminded reader John Crawford: "Years ago I was stopped by a patrol car on Brockburn Road in Pollok. After the usual question, 'Do you know the speed limit here, sir?' which I was well over, I was asked: 'What's the rush?' I said I was late for a meeting with a buyer at Babcock's who was a stickler for punctuality. Said the cop, 'Well, sir, if you just show him this ticket, he'll see why you're late today.'"

IT'S Orange Walk season, and a police officer once told us that one divisional commander, who was addressing the troops before they escorted an Orange Walk through the streets of Glasgow, told them that any officer marching in time to the band would have to answer to him. "I have to say," the officer told us, "it was really quite difficult not to."

A READER once claimed that his work colleague was stopped late at night by officers who made a quick investigation of his car and told him his rear lights were out. Knowing that had happened before, the driver got out, kicked the rear light nearest to him and they came back on.

The unfazed officer merely told him: "That's fine, sir. Now if you kick the windscreen will your road tax come up to date?"

ALWAYS room for a Chic Murray gag. He once said he was knocked off his feet trying to cross a busy Argyle Street, and a passing police officer who came to help him up told the shaken Chic: "There's a zebra crossing just up the road."

"Well, I hope he's having better luck than me," Chic replied.

OUR tales of workplace meals reminded retired cop David Russell: "A prankster colleague at the old Craigmillar Police Station in Edinburgh removed an egg intended as part of a night-shift fry-up from another cop's container. He then hard-boiled it and replaced it, causing much hilarity when the victim tried to break it into the frying pan.

"The following shift, stifled laughter preceded the poor unfortunate's lead-up to cracking that night's egg, causing him to blurt out: 'You've done it again (several expletives deleted) haven't you?' before throwing it at the wall only to watch all that liquid running down the sides of the messroom."

THE dog branch of Police Scotland put a stunning picture of their German Shepherd Rudi on social media this week and told us: "PD Rudi assisted in the apprehension of a male in Glasgow, wanted for an alleged indecent exposure. That's one for the jail."

Among all the comments from folk praising the dog's action was one dissenter who declared: "Bit hypocritical, unless the dog was wearing Y-fronts. One rule for them, one rule for us."

SAD news that *The Buteman* newspaper is closing after 165 years. We in The Diary will especially miss it as we always had room for its stories from the local police. It once reported: "A female was tracked down by CCTV cameras after a local publican reported the theft of a door curtain from his premises. When police found the female, who gave her name as Superwoman, she was wearing the curtain as a cape. Police discretion was used in this instance and the curtain was restored to its rightful owner."

OUR fake nun stories have brought forth a story about actual nuns. Says Dan Edgar in Rothesay: "Years ago, myself and a colleague, both young police officers in uniform, were visiting a friend in what was then the Bon Secours Hospital in Glasgow's south side. The nursing staff were nuns, who in those far-off days had the most elaborate of headwear, a large, white, almost winged affair. Without warning my colleague fainted, dropping like a stone. After a few moments he came round, being comforted by two nuns. The look of absolute terror on his face was incredible. He explained later that he thought he had died and was 'now in Heaven'. I assured him, as a policeman, that would have probably been unlikely."

OUR story about Airdrie made a slighting reference to neighbouring town Coatbridge. Derek McKay at the Big Tree Bar in Coatbridge counters with: "Our town was a leader in industrialisation and was known for coal and steel. Airdrie was known for stealing coal."

OUR tales of whisky bonds reminds a reader: "In 1974 a fire broke out in the Long John bottling plant in Glasgow's London Road and one of the pipes was severed leading to whisky flowing abundantly. The polis in attendance rallied in providing suitable containers to prevent the amber nectar being wasted – including a case of hot water bottles rescued from lost property."

THE website BabyCentre has announced that the classic pram brand Silver Cross has been voted favourite pram in a poll of parents – albeit in a more modern styling than they used to be. It reminds us of former police officer Harry Morris saying that the young woman employed in one CID office to file case reports wasn't perhaps the sharpest. One day she filed the theft of a Silver Cross pram under the heading Jewellery.

OUR tale of police officers liberating whisky from a bond in their division reminds former cop David Russell who worked in Edinburgh: "Our old sergeant related how as a callow youth in the 1950s his job as junior cop was to collect a container of beer at a brewery on the west of the city then tour the beat police boxes topping up screw-top lemonade bottles with it. To help cover the large distances, he used to jump on the step of a shunting goods loco which travelled right along the route. One night he jumped on the wrong loco, a through freight train, and ended up in the marshalling yards at Portobello, several miles away."

WE asked about courtroom tales, and Robin Mather in Musselburgh says: "My favourite story concerned the lawyer who was pleading for leniency on behalf of his client who had just been found guilty. He suggested that his sentence should be in terms of months rather than years. The judge agreed – and sentenced him to 60 months."

THE *Herald* news story about sites being identified for a possible replacement for Barlinnie Prison prompts our old chum Robert Jeffrey, author of the jail's history, *The Barlinnie Story*, to recall the classic tale: "A chaplain told me about one old lag trusted to make the tea and coffee for meetings. The guy was not hot on hygiene and had to be reminded that doing the dishes meant more than a quick swirl under the cold tap. At the next meeting he arrived with a steaming tray of beverages and asked, 'Who wanted the clean cup?'"

WE have been talking about the nicknames that polis officers give each other and a retired officer tells us: "We had one called the Snowman. He got the name as he frequently dismissed any difficulty with the words, 'S'no ma beat, s'no ma problem.'"

OUR Barlinnie Prison stories reminded a Milngavie reader: "A friend of mine was once a prison visitor. One of the old lags told him, as many of them do, that he was in there for something he didn't do. He then added, 'Wipe off my fingerprints.'"

BEST wishes to the little lad recovering after being bitten by an adder in Inverary. Can't help thinking though that we Scots are easier to scare than previous generations. Oban Police had to put out the warning yesterday: "Can we just clarify that the report of a snake's skin in Creag Bhan today was actually a piece of cardboard packaging and not a snake.

The offending packaging was uplifted by police and disposed of in the paper recycling bin."

THE news story about the financial difficulties of cheap and cheerful retail chain Sports Direct reminds us of the stand-up at Edinburgh Festival Fringe who said: "Just got stopped and had my shopping checked at the door of a Sports Direct store like I was some sort of shoplifter. Trust me – if I was a thief, I'd aim higher."

WE asked about food-at-work stories and Richard Gault sends us the ribald tale: "At Airdrie in 1972 we had a gaffer in the police who every nightshift would have the van crew go to his house where his wife would have left his piece in a bag hanging from the front door. Fed up with this task, one of the cops took action.

"I'm told that the look on the Sergeant's face was priceless when he bit into his roll and found what he thought was a used condom. Condensed milk in a new one, tie knot, and insert into Jake Dalziel the baker's finest roll. No more message-boy jobs – result, as they would say nowadays."

WE mentioned nicknames that only applied to police officers, and a retired officer states: "One shift at our office was called The Ghurkhas – because they never took any prisoners."

13

From the Heart

Yes, we all remember the claim that a Scotsman loved his wife so much he almost told her. Here are some other tales of romance.

TRICKY business, the dating game. A Glasgow reader tells us he heard a young lad tell his mates in the pub: "Whenever I tell a girl I meet that I'm a butcher, most of them turn their noses up. So now I tell them I work with animals. Seems to go down better."

AH, going out on the pull. Irish journalist Aoife-Grace Moore remarked this week: "God grant me the confidence of the man on a stag do in Sligo, who tried to chat me up, and once I told him I was engaged, moved onto my mammy beside me and opened with, 'Is her father in the picture?'"

A GLASGOW reader swears a young chap in his local said: "My girlfriend says I'm not romantic enough and that she wants to be wooed." He then added: "So where am I going to get a ghost costume from?"

SAINT Valentine's Day fast approaching and a reader tells us: "My girlfriend asked if I had something special planned for Valentine's Day. I said I was working on it, and she gave me a big smile. Which is odd, as I thought she'd be upset that I'm having to work on Valentine's Day."

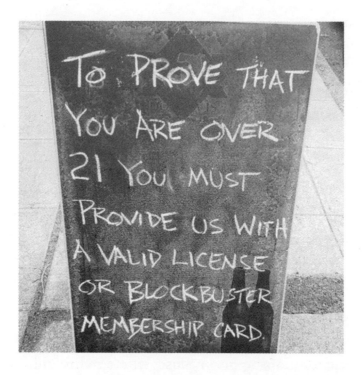

WE mentioned Valentine's Day, and a reader tells us his favourite Valentine's message that he read in a newspaper which printed messages of love on the day was: "Linda B. What are you looking here for? Was dinner and flowers not enough?"

A GLASGOW reader said she heard a chap in a West End bar ask the woman he had been chatting to: "Would you like to swap phone numbers?" But she replied: "No, wouldn't that just confuse people trying to phone me?"

TODAY'S piece of whimsy comes from Victoria Sofia, who declares: "Fun date idea – put a fake diamond ring in your dessert and act like your date proposed. Men love that."

TODAY'S daft gag comes from a Paisley reader who tells us: "A woman I know in the town signed up on one of those dating sites and when asked what she was looking for stated, 'Needs to be good looking, polite, humorous, sporty, knowledgeable, good at singing and dancing. Willing to accompany me the whole day at home during my leisure hours if I don't go out. Be able to tell me interesting stories when I need a companion for conversation and be silent when I want to rest.' They wrote back and told her, 'Buy a television.'"

WE asked about Glasgow discos, and a Jordanhill reader tells us: "I studied at the University of Glasgow in the late 1970s. Friday or Saturday nights were frequently spent at either the Queen Margaret or the Union discos. On one such evening, a fellow female student was being pestered by a regular creep. When asked her name, she replied, 'Annie.' He then pursued this line of questioning and asked her surname.

"'Slandcross' was the answer.

"Her phone number was requested and she provided the number of her local chippie at Anniesland Cross."

SAYS a Glasgow reader: "Imagine trying to impress a younger woman these days by telling her you can rip a phone book in half and she asks you, 'What's a phone book?'"

GOD loves a trier. A reader in a Glasgow pub the other night tells us: "I overheard a guy, trying to chat up a girl, valiantly trying to find out where she was from, and in passing mentions the lovely weather. She says, 'I know, I spoke to my gran earlier who lives near me and she said it was such a nice day.' So, the bloke cleverly asks, 'That's nice. So, where's your gran?' Girl replies, 'Out the back garden.'"

FURTHER back in time a reader recalled an American sailor, on leave from the Polaris submarine base at the Holy Loch, travelling to Glasgow to try his luck at the Locarno Ballroom. The cabbie told him the fare was "seven and six" (7/6d), but the American, unfamiliar with the currency, simply held out a hand bulging with change. The driver picked out half crowns and shillings while explaining: "Seven of those and six of them."

SAINT Valentine's Day saw restaurants busy with couples paying over the odds for a meal because of a few balloons and roses dotted around the place. It does, however, remind us of a case at Greenock Sheriff Court which involved an affray in a local restaurant. A diner who appeared as a witness was asked by the fiscal: "Were you there on a date?"

"No," the chap replied. "I was with the wife."

And a lady having lunch in Glasgow was not impressed by her tired-looking chocolate cake. She sniffed it and declared: "It smells like cocoa."

The smug waiter told her: "It's chocolate cake. It should smell like cocoa."

"Coco's my dog," she replied.

14

Keeping It Healthy

We have to admit that Scots don't have an enviable health record. Amazing really, that they can still joke about it. Here are their recollections.

PEOPLE are still discussing how the Amazon Echo will give medical advice culled from NHS websites. Says Rab Livingstone: "I just asked Alexa where my appendix is. She said, 'Your appendix is in the lower right side of your abdomen.' This is clearly wrong. My appendix is in a bin outside a hospital on the outskirts of Glasgow."

OUR favourite social media comment at the weekend was the chap who declared: "Just saw some idiot at the gym put a water bottle in the Pringles holder on the treadmill."

LATEST research has shown that obese Scots outnumber

smokers by nearly two to one. It reminds us of being at a business lunch in Glasgow where a speaker said she had been at her doctor's for a check-up where she was asked what she weighed. "Eight and a half stone," she replied, but the doc asked her to pop on the scales, and she came in at nine stone, two pounds.

He then asked her height, but after replying five-foot-five, she was asked to stand against a height measuring pole and actually came in at five-foot-three. Doc then took her blood pressure and announced it was a bit on the high side.

"No wonder," she told him. "When I came in here, I was tall and slender. Now I'm short and fat."

GROWING old, continued. A reader tells us: "There is a retired persons golf group where a membership requirement is that they have to be on at least three pills a day."

OUR stories about folk waking up in front of nuns and wondering if they had gone to Heaven brings forth a darker tale from Richard Gault in Dunoon, who says: "In the 1940s when towns had their own gas plants, a relative of mine in Buckie was making his way home in the blackout, but having imbibed somewhat, he fell down the steps into the room where the furnace was just as the furnace-man was stoking up. When he came to, he was startled to see a face peering at him from the smoke and flames.

"The furnace-man asked who he was and he nervously replied: 'When I was alive, I was called Alex.'"

COMMENTS a middle-aged woman: "Pharmacist at the dispensary just asked if I was 36, so I told him I'm actually 45, but have a good skincare regime. Anyway, it turns out he was checking the address on the prescription and was referring to my house number not my age, so if you're looking for a prat I'll be over here."

FOR some reason a reader emails this week's daftest joke:
  Patient: "Do you think me being hard of hearing has contributed to my bird phobia?"
  Doctor: "Maybe a smidgen."
  Patient: "What! Where!?"

A READER phones to tell us: "The TV series *Casualty* is very authentic. It's now in its 33rd series, and I noticed that a punter waiting from series one has just been seen by the doctor."

NOT always a fun day out, visiting the doctor, so we commend the story told to us by journalist John Dingwall who says: "What's been your most absurd medical experience? Mine was today's prostate examination during which the doctor stuck a gloved finger up my backside. At which point all the pound coins I'd stuffed in my pocket to pay for parking fell out of my jeans onto the floor, and I told him he had hit the jackpot."

OUR fascination with all things American continues. We pass on the comment from American Elayne Boosler: "So much of America is so obese now, we're thinking of changing the flag to vertical stripes."

AFTER our tale about NHS websites dumbing down their language in order to be understood, Kate Woods tells us: "Years ago, when my friend was a young girl, she was in hospital and every day the ward sister would ask if her 'bowel had moved'. My friend, not understanding the question and unfamiliar with an Ayrshire accent, thought the sister was saying 'bowl', and as the only bowl she saw was the one her porridge came in she watched intently to see if the bowl moved. As it never did, she always answered 'No', and lived on a daily dose of syrup of figs."

GLASGOW is the second unhealthiest city in the UK new research has announced, with 58% of Glaswegians saying their lifestyles could lead to an early grave. It reminds us of a Glasgow reader who explained to us: "You stand in the queue at Greggs admiring all the healthy salad options, low calorie juices, fruit, yoghurts, spring water, and when they shout 'Next!' for some unexplainable reason you spurt forth with, 'A steak bake, a packet ah cheese an' onion, an' a can ah Irn Bru.'"

And a Glasgow reader once heard a young woman in a coffee shop queue tell her pal: "I don't know whether I should have a cake as well."

And her pal replied: "You're married now. You can eat whatever you want."

OUR hospital stories remind Eric MacDonald: "A friend unfortunately in hospital on New Year's Day was visited by his daughter who brought him in a pre-mixed gin and tonic to celebrate. The mixture was poured into a clear plastic cup and he was enjoying the tipple. Halfway through his drink a nurse came into the room and spotted the cup. She picked it up and poured the contents down the sink, saying, 'I'll just get you some fresh cold water.' Silence!"

STILL struggling with the gym? As Oonagh Keating puts it: "My gym instructor said I should do more resistance train- ing, so I've learnt Morse Code, watched self-defence tutori- als, and I'm memorising the faces of leading Nazis."

A PARTICK reader confessed to us that he started a diet right away after ordering a carry-out from his local Indian restaurant. When he unpacked the food, he noticed the restaurant had included two sets of plastic cutlery rather than one.

AND a Glasgow reader once heard two women discuss a friend who was struggling keeping her weight under control. "She's had her stomach stapled," one confided. "Stapled to what?" asked her pal. "Greggs?"

ST ANDREWS resident Davie Anderson overheard a young waitress being harangued by a party of American tourists in the local hotel bar-bistro. "Are these your only vegetarian dishes?" fumed one tourist, demanding to see a list of vegan food. The waitress confirmed the non-meat options were confined to vegetarian lasagne and veggie-burgers. "But if you don't have a full vegan menu," said the puzzled tourist, "why is this joint called the Dunvegan Hotel?"

Adds Davie: "I predict further disappointment for our colonial cousins, should they visit Saltcoats, Newcastle or Redcar."

15

Shop Till You Drop

Two topics that are often in Scottish conversations – shopping and the weather. Here are some of the tales.

SADLY, with chains such as Tesco taking over the corner shop and the introduction of self-service tills, you don't get so many interactions like this, but as a traveller from Aberdeen commented: "I was in Motherwell, about to get the bus back to Aberdeen. Went into a shoppy and asked for a bottle of water and a Twirl. The man twirled. This is the level of customer service we are sadly lacking in Aberdeen."

WE mentioned supermarket deliveries, and a reader pointed out that getting deliveries from shops is not a new thing, merely reinvented. As entertainer Andy Cameron recalled: "Over 60 years ago most grocer shops had sturdy bikes and even sturdier teenagers who earned a bit of pocket money by delivering a hefty basket full of their merchandise to the 'bought' hooses on the outskirts of Ru'glen. My best pal The Quiet Man did this job for his uncle Jimmy and I was always jealous until one day I saw him pushing the fully laden bike up the brae in Bankhead . . . he was knackered! Those were the days when there was wee shops in every street and with them came the jokes like my granny saying to me, 'Away up tae the butchers and get a sheep's heid for making soup and ask him tae cut it as near the erse as he can.'"

YES, the washing machine can break down at the most inopportune moment. A reader sends us the correct repair procedure for a washing machine going on the blink:

1. Injure your back moving it out from the wall.
2. Gag when you see the disgusting things stuck on the floor where it was.
3. Remove a bit of the machine which you don't know what it does.
4. Watch the kitchen floor fill up with water.
5. Drive to Argos.

IT sounds complicated, but the Scottish Government announced it is going ahead with plans to introduce a deposit scheme of 20p on plastic and glass drinking bottles as well as cans. No doubt grandfathers will be reminiscing with their grandchildren about making a fortune collecting bottles at football grounds after the games – although you had to be careful with any full of a warm liquid. One reader even told us about his local shop only taking back bottles they had sold, and to prove it, would have them stamped with their own sign. Enterprising kids would cut a similar stamp out of a potato, dip it in ink and recreate the sign on any bottle. We think the film *The Great Escape* has a lot to answer for.

ONE of the many downsides of January is making sense of your credit card and bank statements after the free-for-all of Christmas and December. As Neil Reynolds confessed: "This just happened to me! Saw a transaction for £500 to The Body Shop in the bank account. Accused my wife of going mad on shower gel. Then realised it was for the car getting fixed after someone had damaged the paintwork."

TODAY'S piece of whimsy comes from a reader who tells us: "Banks need to get better at restocking these ATMs after Christmas. This is the fifth one I've been to that has 'insufficient funds'."

IT HAS always been tricky for Scots communicating with those whose native tongue is different to their own. A Bellshill reader was in a shop in the famous pilgrimage town of Lourdes in France, where a wee Glasgow wummin was attempting to ascertain the price of rosary beads. Her question: "Whit dae these come in at, hen?" appeared to confuse the shopkeeper somewhat.

WE asked for your porridge tales and a reader reminded us of the tourist at Kelvingrove Art Gallery who asked in the gift shop for a porridge spurtle to buy for someone as a souvenir. The assistant behind the counter said they had none in stock but added: "The Palace might have one. Would you like me to give them a call?" The visitor almost jumped up and down with excitement as she told her pal: "They're going to phone the Palace!" not realising the assistant was referring to the People's Palace over on Glasgow Green.

SOME good weather around the last couple of days. A Knightswood reader tells us: "Have just let my neighbour know that I'm going to sit outside and read for a while. Just to help him be on time with the hedge cutters."

OUR yarn about the gardener putting whisky on his grass brought forward the observation from a few readers, including Peter Hunter, who said: "My neighbour sprays his grass with whisky to save him time and energy because it comes up half cut." Sorry about that.

AND kirk elder Ian Cooper in Bearsden passes on: "There was the apocryphal tale of the new parish minister who stopped at the garden of a non-church attender and declared, 'Good morning, my friend, what a very fine garden you have here – isn't it wonderful what man and God can achieve when working together?'

"'Aye,' retorted the dour gardener, 'But you should've seen the place when God had it to himself.'"

FINALLY, some daftness from a colleague who felt he had to tell us: "My wife and I fell out over what outfits to wear when we start gardening after the weather gets better.

"She's digging in her heels."

YES, the gardening began in earnest at the weekend. Declared Rab Livingstone: "I pulled loads of weeds out of my garden about three weeks ago and now they're back. Here's my question. I actually took them down the tip. They were in a black bin liner tied at the top so they were effectively blindfolded. So how did they know where I live, and how did they get back?"

SOME great weather last week. Says Robert Gardner: "I visited the lovely fishing village, Tarbet, where I popped into the local grocery shop, bought a packet of two empire biscuits, then sat on a bench at the harbour in the sun. I was joined by what I took to be a gentleman of the road. As I demolished a biscuit, I was aware that every bite was being watched. Without saying anything I pushed the other biscuit over to him. He nodded. We both finished at the same time. He nodded again and left. As I packed up one of the locals walked by and said, 'You're the third today.'"

WE know it's a bit of a First World problem, but we did like TV presenter Storm Huntley's social media confession: "Rushed home through Central London to make sure I got home for my Tesco delivery – only to discover I sent it to my old address – in Glasgow."

A GLASGOW reader tells us he was in a bakery where an excitable woman in front of him spotted the cake display and declared to her pal: "I'd kill for a strawberry tart."
The woman behind the counter replied: "We prefer cash."

OUR *Herald* chum Alison Rowat wrote about how to be truly posh. It reminded Duncan Shaw in Kilwinning: "My aunt and uncle lived in Glasgow's West End. In the flat below was a retired doctor who took herself off to Fraser's in Buchanan Street where she made a purchase which was to be delivered the next day. The item arrived, but as she observed, in an Arnott's van. She waited until the men had lugged the box to her door and told them to 'take it back and deliver it tomorrow in a Fraser's van'. Which they did."

16
Transports of Delight

Many Scots have to face public transport on a daily basis, and it throws up some great yarns for The Diary.

NIGEL Manuel, over in Glasgow from New York for his Auntie Maisie's 98th birthday, tells us: "On my last visit home with the missus we took Maisie over to Dunoon on Western Ferries. The ticket guy came to the car and quoted me £19 as the price. Auntie, previously unnoticed in the backseat, pipes up that as a senior citizen she is entitled to a discount. 'That'll be 25 quid then,' said the ticket collector giving the revised price now that he had spotted my aunt. We still laugh about it."

WE pass on the tale from actor Iain Robertson who explained on social media: "I heard a story last night about a pal of mine who used to be a bevy merchant. He got steaming in Glasgow, blacked out and woke up in Vienna, but thought he was in Dundee.

"When ma pal said, 'How did ye think it was Dundee?', he says, 'The buses wur the same colour.'"

A GLASGOW reader swears to us that he was on a Ryanair flight to Spain alongside a group of boisterous lads on a stag weekend. One of the chaps had a seat beside a young woman whom he tried to engage in conversation with the line: "Do Ryanair charge you extra to sit beside a handsome young man?"

"Yes, they do," she immediately responded. "But I wasn't willing to pay it."

A READER told us of an American tourist family driving on to a Scottish pier just after the CalMac ferry had sailed. The father accosted the official on the pier: "Gee, man! We've come all the way from Chicago to catch that ferry!" to which the CalMac man replied: "Well, if you'd left Chicago ten minutes earlier, you would've caught it."

A READER who caught the train to Edinburgh from Glasgow tells us: "I'm beginning to think we were taught the game Musical Chairs as kids in order to prepare us for travelling on ScotRail."

THINGS you can just imagine – we spot a random comment on social media which simply said: "Just seen a bloke in Glasgow trying to hail a driving instructor."

GOOD to see code-breaking computer scientist Alan Turing on the new Bank of England £50 note. A reader on the bus into Glasgow yesterday heard the woman sitting in front of him tell her pal: "I've no idea who this Alan Turing is," before adding: "Mind you, I've no idea what a £50 note is either."

AS the marching season continues, musician Roy Gullane confesses that his band was taken with the fact that there is a Malaysian restaurant in India called the Orange Wok. Once when they were bored in an Asian airport waiting for a flight, they asked the information desk to page: "Rasashma

Farrawoar from the Orange Wok." Well, it helped pass the time.

FRANCES Woodward was on a train to Falkirk when the recording came over the Tannoy system telling passengers what to do if they see anything suspicious, followed by the "See it, say it and we'll sort it" mantra. The ScotRail chap selling tickets looked up from his ticket machine and announced: "Dinnae come tae me, I've goat ma trainers on and will be running in the opposite direction."

THE Scottish Government is putting the debt-ridden Prestwick Airport up for sale after discovering that buying it for a pound a few years ago wasn't such a good bargain. We recall one reviewer a while back declaring it was a great place to sleep overnight without being disturbed, although he was asked by the security chap who was heading out for a short while if he could let the cleaner in if she arrived. Another recent reviewer was less impressed declaring: "Prestwick Airport is essentially a very fancy bus stop, but £7.99 to Portugal is a no-brainer. Food is tasty enough but extortion for what it is – burger and fish and chips cost literally more than the train from Glasgow and the flights combined."

OUR mention of bus conversations in Glasgow made Maureen McRoberts in Hamilton recall: "Years ago while travelling on a very crowded bus, a friend further back shouted over to me, 'Aye your boy has been in there plenty of times.' We were passing Barlinnie Prison at the time, but he had failed to add that my boy was a criminal lawyer interviewing his clients. To this day I will never forget the look of sheer horror and disquiet on the lady sitting next to me. She actually stood up and found another seat."

AH, the banter on trains to Glasgow. Tom Rafferty was journeying from Ayr to Glasgow early on Saturday evening when he noticed that a few of the young folk were consuming alcoholic beverages – "prees" as they are known in common parlance, as in pre the more expensive pubs you are going to later. Says Tom: "The ticket collector was polite with the boys opposite me, who have cider and Mad Dog on the go, and who asked for 'three halfs to Glasgow'. He looked at the table and told them, 'Pay full fare or I'll need to take that cargo off you.'"

POINT to ponder from reader Graham Livingstone: "A bit concerning to note from a communication offering my wife car insurance that, 'If you require this in large print or Braille please let us know.'"

SOMETIMES social media conversations can be enlightening. Chris Godfrey, travelling from London to Aberdeen, went online to sigh: "My boyfriend was in charge of supplies for the four-and-a-half-hour train journey to Scotland we are currently on. For this journey – standing the whole time by the way – he has bought no bottles of water, two cans of gin and tonic, one pack of chicken satay and one tube of sour cream and onion Pringles."

Scots lass Ange Fitpatrick replied: "Maybe you'll get lucky. I was on a very delayed train to Glasgow, standing between carriages. The trolley got to us and couldn't go any further. Businessman next to me bought the lot on his company card – wine and beer for the adults, sweets for the kids. Impromptu train party!"

BUS company First Glasgow has announced that it will be putting three of their buses out on the road in the classic paint liveries of Glasgow Corporation in the 1960s, Glasgow PTE in the 1970s and Strathclyde Buses in the 1980s to mark the 125th anniversary of public transport in the city. By memory we reckon that will be green and yellow, white, green and yellow, and orange.

Our favourite Glasgow Corpy bus story is the one the late, great Chic Murray told: that when he was a schoolboy, he was on the top deck of a Corpy bus with his father when the bus performed an abrupt emergency stop.

Passengers were thrown forwards, and Chic recalled: "I was uninjured, but fortunately my father had the presence of mind to throw me down the stairs."

A CHIC Murray debate! Our mention of the Glasgow Subway reminds readers of the late great Chic arriving at

Hillhead station to ask if the next train had a buffet car. When told no, he merely replied he would just wait for the next one then. Entertainer Andy Cameron gets in touch to claim that Chic, when told there were no buffet cars, replied: "Christ! I'll be starving by the time I get to Merkland Street." We suspect that both versions are correct as we are sure Chic used that line more than once.

MORE on the Glasgow Subway as retired Eaglesham scout leader Alistair Moss tells us that he took a troop of Beaver Scouts – that's the younger lads – on a tour of the system in the early 1990s.

Says Alistair: "My friend in charge allowed each Beaver to drive the train for two stations round the inner circle until they all had a shot. On arriving at Cowcaddens two women were on the platform and noticed a six-year-old boy in the driver's seat with one of them commenting, 'They're so short of staff they're using weans!'"

OUR story about the old bus colours in Glasgow being revived reminds Hugh Steele in Cumbernauld: "One of the girls in our office came in one day with an orange top and a green skirt. The office wag said, 'You look like a Corpy bus dressed like that.' Her reply was, 'Aye, but ye'll no get jumpin' on me fer one and six.'

"It's ancient, I know, and you might have to explain what one and six was." No Hugh, not to Diary readers we don't.

REALLY sad news that the paddle steamer *Waverley* is unable to sail this year as it needs new boilers. We recall author Meg Henderson being on Arran when the *Waverley* docked and a tipsy passenger asked where the bookies were.

Said Meg: "We explained that there was no bookies. He looked shocked. 'So wherra boozer?' We said the pubs would be shut at that moment. He shook his head. 'Wherra chip shoap?' We said there was no chippie. The day tripper yelled, 'That boat's brung me tae Hell!' and he staggered back up the gangway."

GOODNESS, we read it is 50 years since Concorde first flew – time flies, which is more than you can say for Concorde these days. We liked the story about comedian Bob

Hope's first trip on the sleek plane which was admittedly a little on the cramped side.

He took one look at the little toilet and told the stewardess: "You really have to decide what you're gonna do before going into one of these. Either reverse in, or forward, for us guys."

A GARAGE manager told us that a customer brought in his car which had two side panels bashed in, and told the mechanic that he was driving in the country when it was hit by "a herd of horses".

The mechanic looked puzzled and told him: "Herd of horses? Is it not a herd of cows?"

But the customer replied: "Naw, it was definitely horses."

AN English chap working in Glasgow told his colleagues in the pub: "I got a train to Airdrie the other night. The ticket chap said it would be 19.45 when we arrived.

"He was being a bit harsh – it looked more like the early 1960s to me."

WE love the sheer poetry of former Communards multi-instrumentalist turned vicar, the Rev Richard Coles, who wrote on social media this week: "Whenever I take the Sleeper to Glasgow I wake up and open my window and discover we're behind Iceland in Motherwell, and I watch the rats scampering around and think, 'You don't see that on a tin of shortie.'"

A READER passes on the comment from the driver on the bus from Inverness to Glasgow who announced: "Please listen carefully to the following announcement. For your comfort, safety and convenience I would advise you that I have a special name for anyone who smokes or drinks alcohol on my bus. I call them pedestrians. Enjoy your journey and thank you for travelling with us today."

OUR ferry stories remind Mike Jarron: "Visited Gigha some years ago, and the little vehicle ferry had hardly started out from Tayinloan when it swung around and lowered its loading ramp. This was a bit worrying, thinking about what happened to the *Herald of Free Enterprise* when it failed to raise its ramp. The ferry then went back and forth a few yards swinging about each time. Turned out the skipper was trying to line up on a floating object, the crew's football, which had been lost overboard so that it would be swept up the ramp.

"After several attempts, to the cheers of the passengers, the ball was retrieved by a crew member wielding a broom. That trip took about twice as long as scheduled."

ALWAYS interesting, the chats with taxi drivers at this time of year – although it is the only occupation where we can't stop ourselves from asking: "So what time are you on till?" Anyway, a south side reader was heading home from the city centre the other night when his chatty taxi driver told him he had a PhD – then added it stood for "Pot-Hole Dodging".

READER Sandy Tuckerman passes on the story from musician Phil Cunningham about when his sports car was set on fire by thieves many years ago in their frustration at not being able to get it started.

Says Sandy: "The police arrived promptly and while they surveyed the smouldering wreck in Edinburgh's Gorgie one of the officers asked him what make it was. Phil told him it was an MGB GT. To ensure his notes were accurate the constable asked, 'Could you spell that please?'"

THERE has always been the dodge when you arrive at Glasgow Central station without a ticket to simply say you got on at the last stop and buy a ticket from there. We read a chap on social media this week explain: "Tried tae get a ticket on the train in Central n say as fay Paisley, n the guy asked me wir ma postcode wis. Wow man, new level a jobsworth."

AH, public transport at this time of year. Nicki on social media declares: "You don't know what fun is until you've witnessed a drunk on the Edinburgh to Glasgow train screaming, 'Ah hate hedgehogs – come at me ya jabby wee ****' while angrily circling a hairbrush that's been dropped on the floor."

IF THE GROUND GETS TOO CLUTTERED WITH CIGARETTE BUTTS, PLEASE FEEL FREE TO USE THE ASHTRAYS

GROWING old continued. It says much for the age of the fellow passengers that when reader Jim Morrison returned from a five-day coach trip to Yorkshire with a coachload of Scottish pensioners, the driver announced on the last day: "Now we are heading for home, I hope you have not forgotten anything like yer specks or yer hearing aid or yer wig or yer false teeth, glass eye or widden leg as we are not back here later, thank you."

17

Chosen at Random

Some stories are just too difficult to categorise. Here are a few at random.

RELIGIOUS thought for the day by actor Matt Lucas, who observes: "Whenever I meet those evangelical types in the street and they start talking about the Bible and how Christ died for my sins, I just say, 'No spoilers please! I'm still only on the bit where he's feeding the 5,000.'"

PAISLEY meat-market worker John Sword recalled a colleague who told everyone of the drama of his chip pan going on fire the previous night and the fire brigade being called out to save their house. He had reached the point in his tale where he said that the family dog had gone for the fireman when an astonished listener, presumably brought up on too many Lassie films, asked: "Your dog ran all the way to the fire station?"

"Naw," explained the chap. "He went for the first fireman through the door and sank his teeth into him."

MULTI-MILLIONAIRE Richard Branson, possibly spending too long in the sun at his exclusive own island, declared on social media: "I truly believe that 'stuff' really does not bring happiness. Family, friends, good health and the satisfaction that comes from making a positive difference are what really matters." A cynical Sarah Phelps quickly replied: "Gie's yer stuff then."

JUST to cheer you up, we pass on the doggy story from broadcaster Lucy Freeman who was out for a walk and observed: "Saw a Labrador in the river, appearing to struggle. It was whining and complaining. I drew the attention of its owner who said, 'He's always doing this. Bloody drama queen. Joe! Put your feet down!' The Labrador looks sheepish and stands up – in water which comes up to its knees."

A COLLEAGUE wanders over with that look on his face that says he has a terrible joke to tell me. "Saw a neighbour nick socks off our washing line," he bellows before adding: "Was going to confront him, but I got cold feet."

TODAY'S piece of daftness comes from Gary Delaney, who says: "I was staying at a friend's and he said, 'I'll make up the spare room,' and he was true to his word. There was no spare room."

DOG owners will no doubt agree with Liz Hackett who points out: "Having an older dog means ten seconds after you drop a piece of food, you have to drop an even bigger piece of food so they can find it."

SOMEHOW we got onto discussions about what is worse – a cold public toilet seat or a warm one. A reader gets in touch: "On the old Merchant Navy cadet training ship

Conway during cold weather, which was almost all the time, the senior cadets would send junior cadets to warm the toilet seats before the senior ones used them."

And another reader observed: "Some women I know only took up yoga so that they could flush public toilets with their feet."

AS Burns Night approaches we hear from Dundee where former MP Jim McGovern gave the Toast to the Lassies at the local Labour Party Burns Supper. His wife Norma gave the reply with the great opening line: "When I realised I was speaking right after Jim, I thought, 'Jim is used to public speaking, he'll be a hard act to follow.' Thankfully I was wrong!"

AND our story about the Rev James Currie being known as the Thief of Bad Gags for copying down lines from other Burns Supper speakers reminds Ian Young: "As an inveterate note-taker myself, when attending dinners, of other speakers' jokes for my later use, I have long been aware of the possible admonition from the top table speaker of, 'Am I speaking slowly enough for you?' To fend this off, I have developed my own ready response of, 'Oh, I'm not writing them down, I'm ticking them off.'"

WE mentioned the great Burns speaker the Rev James Currie. As a reader once recalled: "In one Immortal Memory he told of taking his car to a garage for a service – the Burns connection evades me – and he said to the mechanic, 'Don't charge me too much, I'm just a poor minister.' The mechanic replied, 'Aye, ah ken. I heard you on Sunday.'"

TODAY'S piece of daftness comes from Craig Deeley who says: "My friend never knew the difference between 'infer' and 'imply'. It never really mattered until he opened a club called Disco Implyno."

A BEARSDEN reader tells us she was round at a friend's house when her pal referred to one of the rooms as "the panic room". This bemused our reader who asked: "What, one of those panic rooms that rich people have to hide in if they come under attack?"

"No," said her pal, "A panic room where you throw all the clutter in quickly when someone arrives at your house unexpectedly."

IT'S the quick reactions of people that can make social media comments so entertaining. As a young woman named Kelsey in California wrote the other day: "One time I hit a squirrel with my car and cried about it for two hours. What are you all thinking about today?"

Within minutes someone had replied: "My missing pet squirrel . . ."

18

Technically Speaking

We have to admit it, technology is changing our lives at such a fast rate. Here is how our readers have been coping.

WE can imagine a few folk sympathising with a husband who commented the other day: "My wife has this app on her phone that notifies her the second I've finished checking out at the supermarket, so that she can then text and ask me to pick up one more thing."

DAFT gag of the day from a reader who emails: "My mate is so engrossed with technology he got a mobile phone implanted into his throat. When his mum finds out she's going to ring his neck."

PROBLEMS that new technology brings with it. Says James Hinton: "The fingerprint scanner on my smartphone doesn't work if your finger is too warm, too cold, pressed down lightly or pressed down too hard. It's the Goldilocks of phones."

A READER swears he heard a young woman on the train into Glasgow the other day tell her pal: "I forgot my phone when I went to the bathroom this morning. Did you know we've got 84 tiles on the bathroom wall?"

DAFT remark from a reader who tells us: "Went on to a shopping site that asked me to put in a password so I put 'chicken'. It then said, 'Password must contain a capital.' So I put 'chickenkiev'."

THE anniversary of the first moon landing gave us all food for thought. We liked the comment of economics professor William Easterly who remarked: "Our smartphones are 120 million times more powerful than the computers that guided *Apollo 11*. That has enabled us to progress from moon landings to cat videos."

RECALLING the moon landing, Brian Donohoe in Ayrshire told us: "We were on holiday staying with my uncle – a canon in the Church of England – who didn't have a TV so we listened on the radio, which was not so exciting. He had set up four glasses and a bottle of Drambuie for when the landing took place, and as we sat waiting for the momentous event which eventually happened at approximately 3 a.m. I kept thinking I had never waited as long for a drink in my life."

AND Glasgow actor Gavin Mitchell recalled: "I actually remember watching the moon landing, I even remember what I was wearing – it was a nurse's uniform free with *Twinkle*, a girls' comic. This consisted of a plastic Red Cross apron and hat. And I kept trying to administer treatment to my big brother who was lying on the couch trying to watch the event as I got in his way. I always had a sense of theatricality, gender fluidity, pushing my range . . . and being bloody annoying."

WE asked about your memories of the moon landing, and Brian Collie said: "I had the busiest newspaper pitch in Priesthill at the corner of Peat Road and Priesthill Road. I used to sell about 300 papers each day from 6 a.m. to 8.45 a.m. On the Monday following the moon landing I slept in as I'd been up all night and 14-year-olds need a good 12 hours, as we can all understand. I trooped up to collect my papers at 9.30 a.m. and there was not a soul in sight, so took them all home and sold one to my mammy and one to the wee woman next door.

"When the paper man came to collect my spares, he was apoplectic and shouted that this was the biggest story of our lifetimes and I'd only sold two ******* papers!"

THE news that the voice-operated gadget the Amazon Echo will now answer your medical questions with information from NHS sites is not regarded by everyone as a good thing. Writer Aaron Gillies tries to imagine such a scenario and writes:
"Alexa . . . my heart."
"*Playing Achy Breaky Heart.*"
"No . . . I'm having a heart attack."
"*Art Attack is a 90s children's TV show . . .*"
"Alexa, my arm is sore."
"*New alarm set for four.*"

"Alexa, for the love of God call me an ambulance."

"Thank you, I will now refer to you as an ambulance."

MORE on memories of the moon landing as a reader reminds us that it was said that when Neil Armstrong, the first man on the moon, went on a speaking tour discussing his exploits, he always used the line, if he told a joke about his moon exploits and it didn't get a laugh: "Guess you had to be there."

WE asked for your stories about the moon landing and a Hillhead reader confessed: "As a small boy I was allowed to stay up very late to watch it on the telly. I'm embarrassed to admit that after watching the grainy pictures I told my parents that it 'wasn't as good as *Star Trek*', which I had seen for the first time just a week earlier."

WE have mentioned how new electronic devices are chang-ing the way we act around the house. As writer Nick Bilton revealed: "My four-year-old son, who has grown up watching us talk to Siri and Alexa, thinks you can talk to anything that has a screen or is plugged into the wall. This morning he told the toaster to order him a new Lego set."

MANY folk are enjoying their Amazon Echos, but not everyone is a fan. As a Lynn Anderson left as her review on Amazon: "Forget it – especially if you have a Scottish accent.

You'll spend the whole time becoming increasingly frustrated, swearing at it, bawling at it, then trying to stop yourself hurling it right oot the windae! Meantime your neighbours are calling the polis, thinking that someone is being murdurred upstairs. And they are right. It's that bloody Alexa."

19

Gone But Not Forgotten

Here we are fondly remembering people who left us in the past year.

EVERY football fan will be saddened by the death of Billy McNeill who had such a commanding presence when you met him. Most of us know the story that Billy's original nickname was "Cesar" after actor Cesar Romero but it morphed into "Caesar" when Celtic won the European Cup. Journalist Alex Gordon, who compiled the book *Billy McNeill: In Praise of Caesar* checked with Billy's wife Liz which she preferred and she gave the touching reply: "I'm not fussed. I've never had to write either on a Christmas or birthday card. I've always called my husband Billy."

WE recall Billy at a *Herald* book event telling the audience that the basic wage when Celtic won the European Cup in

1967 was 40 quid a week. The next year, the players sent Captain Billy in to see formidable manager Jock Stein about a rise.

Says Billy: "I eventually came back to the players and told them, 'Well I did my best, but you know what the Big Man's like, no chance.' The real story is that I went in, said the lads thought they were due a wage rise, and Big Jock said, 'F**k off.' There was no point in arguing with him. I then went and sat in the toilet for half an hour so that the lads would think we had at least had meaningful negotiations."

BILLY was of course both captain and later manager of Celtic. Former goalie Peter Latchford told the story that when Billy was appointed Celtic manager, he got the players together to tell them that there was now a divide between him and the players. He went on at length about how he was no longer "Big Man" or whatever, and that he was now "The Manager" or even "Mr McNeill". At the end of his speech he asked if there were any questions and Danny McGrain replied: 'No, I think you covered all the bases, Billy.'"

FURTHER cruel news with the death of Stevie Chalmers so soon after that of Billy McNeill. Stevie served his two years' National Service in the RAF before becoming a Celtic player and was once given a lift home to Glasgow in a jet fighter from Suffolk. As he later memorably recalled: "Nervousness was affecting me so much that I was moved to ask the pilot via the microphone in my headset what would happen if my ejector button would not work. He responded that he would simply tip the plane on its side, ping open the Perspex hatch and tip me out. That only added to my misgivings and I vomited violently and copiously in the aircraft. It was the only flight I took in my two years of service."

SAD to hear of the death of musician and cartoonist Malky McCormick, whose caricatures of folk famous and not-so-famous have adorned newspapers and even pub walls for many years. Malky always had a wicked sense of humour. He once told me that in his first office job in Glasgow he had to go out for the lunches folk ordered, and one boss was always complaining about the food.

So, the young Malky bought a plastic fried egg from Tam Shepherd's joke shop, put it in a roll, complete with hot oil over it, and put it amongst the lunchtime orders. The ever-complaining recipient took one bite, declared it the worst fried egg ever, and stomped off to the shop to complain as Malky told the rest of the office what he had done.

SUCH sad news that Rony Bridges, scriptwriter, actor, gallery owner, pub manager and more recently charity organiser, has died. Starchild, which he organised with his lovely partner Michaela Foster Marsh, has helped build and run a school in Uganda which has more than 100 pupils. His other big success was when he wrote *Six and a Tanner*, a moving play about growing up in Springburn with an alcoholic domineering father. It was put on at Greenock Prison, and afterwards a chuffed Rony told actor Tony Roper: "One lifer told me it was the most powerful piece of drama he had ever seen."

"To be fair," replied Tony cautiously, "he probably doesn't get out much."

BRIAN Pendreigh's obituary of Rony Bridges in *The Herald* explained how a working-class lad from Springburn stumbled into acting. It reminded us of when Rony himself once told us: "What a week. Urgently needed a plumber and a tiler, but all too busy so went to a play in the West End. Who is in the audience? Our tiler. Who's in the play? Our plumber!"

AMERICAN actor Rip Torn from *The Larry Sanders Show* and the first *Men in Black* movies has died at the age of 88. I remember a film buff on *The Herald* once telling me that Rip was supposed to play the role Jack Nicholson made famous in *Easy Rider* but pulled out as the salary wasn't big enough to pay a tax bill he had.

Fellow *Easy Rider* star Dennis Hopper later claimed on a chat show that Rip had been sacked after pulling a knife on him. Rip sued, a witness came forward to say that it was Hopper who pulled a knife, and Rip was awarded damages of half a million dollars – more than 100 times the fee he was offered.

THE death of ebullient former TV racing tipster John McCririck reminds us of when he was hired to make a cameo appearance in the Scottish comedy series *Still Game*. John arrived for filming at a race day at Lingfield Park, looked around, and declared there were not enough punters there to make it look busy and suggested they go for lunch first. After a very long and very enjoyable lunch – courtesy of the BBC of course – John finally agreed there was enough of a crowd and went out to be filmed.

Please note:
The post-apocalyptical
fiction section
has been moved to
Current Affairs.

WE mentioned the late racing tipster John McCririck, and a Motherwell reader tells us: "John was never short of a word or three when he was on the telly but I do remember when he was once completely silenced. He was commenting at the Prix de l'Arc de Triomphe in Paris when there was a photo finish.

"As they were waiting for the result, John heard a bing-bong from the public address system and told viewers: 'Here's the result now.' It was of course given in French and John just stood there open-mouthed as you realised his brain was trying to get round a foreign language."

AND reader Gerry MacKenzie tells us: "A good few years back John turned up in Milngavie town centre to do the opening honours for a new branch of one of the big national bookmaker's chains. He regaled the assembled punters with amusing stories, cut the tape and then advised them to stash every penny they had in their possession on a nag he named, due to race in 20 minutes' time. He assured them it was a 'dead cert'. The punters did so. The nag coasted it. The new manager was sick as the proverbial parrot."

SAD to hear of the sudden death of Scots golfer Gordon Brand Junior who played for Europe in the Ryder Cup and won eight titles before becoming a regular on the senior circuit. On his first year as a senior he was in a play-off at Slaley Hall when he was put off by a mobile phone ringing and scored an eight on a par three. He couldn't complain too much, however – it was his own phone.

THE death has been announced of the former Roman Catholic Archbishop of Motherwell, Joe Devine. Joe could be quite a hardliner on some of his views but we did like what he wrote in a letter to *The Herald* after criticism of Tony Blair joining the Catholic Church. After acknowledging some of the faults of Labour Party policies at the time, Joe added: "It is regrettable that some would have Mr Blair walk barefoot in sackcloth and ashes and make a public recantation of his sins. That being the case, I would in similar fashion have to follow alongside him and so would everyone else I know. It would be quite a procession."

JUDITH Kerr, the great children's book author and illustrator, has died at the age of 95. She cheerily told *The Herald* last year that she had a 'Do Not Resuscitate' notice signed by her doctor which she kept in her hall, and explained: "Sometimes I feel like sticking it on the front door, but that's a bit much and a bit depressing for visitors."

She then added with a smile: "Somebody said that the only way is to have 'Do Not Resuscitate' tattooed on your chest. But I never know exactly how to spell 'resuscitate'."

THE sad news yesterday was the death of former World Champion racing driver Niki Lauda, whose duels with James Hunt were legendary. The story about Niki getting into racing was that his family had sent him to college where he wasn't faring well.

In the end he took home a college diploma from a girlfriend on which he had printed his name over his girlfriend's and flashed it towards his mum and dad without letting them actually hold it. His delighted dad wrote him a cheque as a reward for passing his college exam, and Niki promptly went out and bought a car with it.

THE death of veteran singer Doris Day reminds us of an interview Doris gave when her last album came out a few years ago and she said: "I feel so fortunate that I was able to do something I loved so much. I would have worked for nothing, and I really mean it." She then added after a slight pause: "My mother once said to me, 'Don't tell anyone that.'"

SIR David McNee, who has sadly died, was involved in high-profile events as Metropolitan Police Commissioner, but there were humbler cases when he was a beat bobby in Glasgow's Partick – such as the time he booked 16 youths for playing football at four in the morning. He felt the noise was unfair on folk trying to sleep, but knowing they might simply run away he gathered up their jackets which they had put down for goals. As they queued up for their jackets, he booked them, apart from one jacket-less lad who ran away.

Constable McNee followed him home where he was hiding in the staircase cludgie. As David dragged him off, the lad's mother attacked David in the street with such ferocity her nightgown fell off, with the lad shouting: "Look what you've done to my mam!"

BEFORE he joined the police, Sir David was called up during the war to the Navy as a teenager and was sent for training to Skegness. He later recalled: "It wasn't profitable to complain about the food. I did so once when I found a cockroach in my soup only to be told sharply by the petty officer of the day, 'McNee, hush your mouth. You have more meat in your soup than anyone else.' I finished the soup and never complained again."

THE *Herald* news story that Scottish libraries now have fewer computers in order to save money reminds us somehow of the librarian, when asked for the most unusual reason for a lost library book, said a woman offered to pay for a book she had borrowed as she had used it to prop up the head of her recently departed husband for an open coffin viewing, and had then forgotten to remove it before he was cremated.

FOOTBALL fans are mourning the passing of stalwart Rangers and Scotland captain Eric Caldow. Entertainer Andy Cameron recalls: "Eric was a lovely man. Many years after he missed the penalty in the 1961 Cup Winners Cup

Final I was sitting at a Rangers do when somebody came up and asked him why the referee had allowed the Fiorentina goalkeeper to come so far off his line before the kick was taken and Eric told him, 'I don't ken why, but if the goalie had been any closer I'd have thought he fancied me.'"

A POSTSCRIPT on the sad death of Prodigy singer Keith Flint whose biggest hit with the band was 'Firestarter'. In later years Keith was the licensee of his local pub in Essex, the Leather Bottle, which had an open fire. Keith explained that whenever he went to put coal on the fire and any customer who thought it would be funny to start singing 'Firestarter' would be told to put a pound in the charity box on the mantelpiece. It raised nearly £100.

SAD to hear of the death of former Radio Clyde breakfast host Mike Riddoch, one of the cleverest DJs around, although he hated being in the spotlight himself. He once told an old chum of ours that he didn't like to sound too bright and breezy in the morning as it put folk off if they had just woken up. He added: "The greatest compliment I've ever had is from someone who once said he liked me because 'however rough I feel, Mike Riddoch seems to be feeling rougher'."

OUR mention of plans to create a memorial to the late miners' leader Mick McGahey reminds Dan Edgar in Rothesay: "My sadly departed friend, the late, great Jimmy Reid, once told me about enjoying a dram with Mick in a London pub after a busy day of union business. Two whiskies arrived on their table. McGahey complained to the barman, 'There's a fly in my glass'. The barman apologised profusely with McGahey replying, 'The fly is no really the problem – the fact that it can walk aboot is!'"

WE have been remembering the late Scottish miners' leader Mick McGahey as there is talk of having a permanent memorial to him. As Paul O'Sullivan recalls: "During the miners' strike in 1984, the NUM had a meeting with the National Coal Board headed by Ian McGregor. As they were coming out of the meeting, McGregor put a plastic bag over his head to avoid being photographed. Mick asked him, 'Taken up glue-sniffing, huv ye?'"

SADDEST news yesterday was the death of chef Andrew Fairlie who not only ran the country's best restaurant, but did it with warmth and friendliness. He was also a great Celtic fan, as we remember from a reception at the Balmoral Hotel in Edinburgh when he had one of his rare nights away from his restaurant in Gleneagles to receive the Walpole Medal of Excellence. Andrew told guests at the ceremony that he was glad there was a photographer recording the event as his staff were convinced he had made the presentation up so he could bunk off to watch a Celtic European tie.

A BEARSDEN reader once told us about the organist at a funeral he attended playing the rousing Dambusters March as the mourners were leaving the crematorium. When the undertaker asked why he chose the music the organist rather smugly replied that he had noticed that the deceased had a floral arrangement spelling out Biggles and assumed that was his nickname as a former RAF pilot. The undertaker shook his head and told him: "You were half correct. It was a nickname – he was known as Big Les."

THE death of singer Leon Redbone who had such a rich, mellow voice, reminds a reader of attending one of his concerts at the Queen's Hall in Edinburgh. Leon liked to chat to the audience between numbers, and he told those present about his difficulties in sleeping: "My doctor told me to drink whisky an hour before bedtime," he exclaimed, before adding, "I could only manage to do it for 45 minutes before I had to give up as I couldn't drink anymore."

BBC newsreader Richard Baker has died at the age of 93. He wrote in his biography about the shock of newsreaders becoming personalities and being stopped in the street by the public who asked for autographs. He did add, though, that once in Glasgow someone in the street saw him and cried: "It is! It's no'!" The fan then reached the loud conclusion: "It is! Wee fatty!"

SAD to hear of the death of former *Herald* columnist and broadcaster Kenneth Roy who went on to set up the challenging but always readable *Scottish Review*. Once writing about why he left BBC Scotland in the *Review*, Kenneth stated: "One day, in the lavatory at the end of the corridor, I watched one of my colleagues – a nice man in early middle age – popping pills to control his stress. A year later he was dead. That might have been a catalyst: the realisation that, if there were causes worth dying for, *Reporting Scotland* wasn't one of them."

FORGOT to mention that Partick Thistle legend, the frequently sent-off Chic Charnley, was at the launch of the Billy McNeill tribute book, *In Praise of Caesar* in Glasgow. Chic, although a great Celtic fan, was never signed by the club and he confesses: "I cornered Billy McNeill one night at a sporting function. 'Why have you never signed me for Celtic?' I asked, cutting to the chase. Big Billy didn't even blink an eye. 'There's a very good reason for that Chic, son,' he answered. 'I like to sleep at night.'"

THE other sad news was the death of French crooner Charles Aznavour at the age of 94. Glasgow accountant-turned-comedian Arnold Brown told the story that, when he was asked for confirmation of his identity in a branch of his bank, he told the cashier to phone his home branch. She did so, being informed that the account-holder in question looked like Charles Aznavour.

Said Arnold: "So I started singing and convinced them I was Arnold Brown."

BRITAIN'S biggest funeral company, Co-op Funeralcare, has released its 2019 Funeral Music Chart, which sees Frank Sinatra's 'My Way' as the most requested song to be played at funerals. What draws our interest is that the Co-op also gives the Top Ten of other musical genres including rock music, which appears to attract a peculiar set of people. The most requested rock number is, fair enough, Led Zep's 'Stairway to Heaven', but also in the rock top ten is 'Bat Out of Hell', AC/DC's 'Highway to Hell' and the splendid Queen anthem 'Another One Bites the Dust'.

20

A Sporting Chance

Most Scots might not be that fit, but they do love a sporting tale or two.

THE news story about the statue being unveiled to Lisbon Lion Bobby Lennox reminds a Diary chum: "The charity side Dukla Pumpherston were playing down south, and on the bus somebody suggested that Bobby entertain the company. A Rangers player bet Bobby that he couldn't sing 'The Sash'. 'Of course, ah can,' says Bobby and started, *'Sure it's old and it is beautiful,'* then stopped. He then explained, 'That's all ah know because at that point we always scored, and the Rangers supporters shut up.'"

FORMER rugby star Doddie Weir, whose autobiography *My Name'5 Doddie* is now a bestseller, was speaking in Galashiels about the book which details his career and coping with Motor Neurone Disease. Doddie, who has a farm nearby, took questions from the audience at the event, and after the first two questions about Borders rugby rivalry and playing for the Lions, he then realised how special the Borders can be.

The third question was from a local who asked: "Why did you no' buy any sheep from me this year?"

FORMER Celtic and St Mirren star Frank McAvennie, at the launch of old St Mirren mate Billy Abercromby's autobiography, told of the time Aber turned up at a club night out in Glasgow wearing a sheepskin jacket and slippers.

Said Frank: "When we asked Billy why he was wearing slippers, he told us he had been walking his dog and had suddenly remembered about the night out. He then legged it straight from his dog-walking to the nightclub, and when we asked where the dog was, Billy said he just put it on the bus and asked the driver to let it off at the next stop."

A GLASGOW reader gets in touch to tell us: "When I saw the headline on the BBC website's sports pages 'Colombian cyclist wins Tour de France', I thought to myself that after so many years of scandal in the sport, it was a relief to see a winner nobody would suspect of drug offences."

OUR stories about getting golf lessons reminded David Stubley: "Some years ago I went for a lesson with the golf pro at my club. After watching me hit balls for about ten minutes he said: 'Your problem is that your clubs are better than your golf.'"

MORE on getting golf lessons as Boyd Houston in Dollar tells us: "A sadly now-late friend and neighbour, a very heavily busted lady, reported after her first golf lesson that the professional told her: 'Mrs McFarlane, you either play over them or under them, you cannot play through them.'"

GREAT to see Ireland's Shane Lowry out celebrating his Open Championship win by taking the famous Claret Jug with him to the pub – makes a change from American winners having one glass of Budweiser before getting on their private jet.

We also liked his lovely old gran being interviewed on Irish television and recalling: "I remember his grandfather, after he won the Mulling Scratch Cup, saying: 'Get out there and bring me in a bucket of turf.' He said: 'You won't see Tiger Woods bringing in turf.' He thought he was Tiger Woods when he won the Mulling Scratch Cup! Ah great days."

TALKING of golf, an Ayrshire reader emails: "A woman here in Troon was taking her first golf lesson. She asked the instructor, 'I was just wondering, is the word spelled p-u-t or p-u-t-t?'

'P-u-t-t is correct,' he told her. 'P-u-t means to place

something where you want it. P-u-t-t means merely a vain attempt to do the same thing.'"

OUR tales of bad golf shots reminded entertainer and enthusiastic golfer Andy Cameron: "I played with former Open champion Sandy Lyle in the Glasgow Classic at Haggs Castle once and after several nervous practice swings I decided to shut my eyes and let fly. 'Can you see it Sandy?' I enquired. 'See it? I can reach it,' said Sandy.

"And my good friend Jim Cullen who owned the Montrose Bar asked me as I came into the clubhouse at Cathkin Braes after a medal how I got on. I shook my head and declared, 'Ninety-eight, a bad day at Black Rock.'

"'Ye must have putted well,' was his less-than-sympathetic observation."

OUR favourite old golf gag – a regular golfer would go out every Saturday morning at seven to play a round come rain, hail or shine. But one weekend when he reached the door, the biting cold rain was almost horizontal, and for once he put his golf bag down, undressed and quietly slipped back into bed with his half-asleep wife and told her: "The weather's terrible."

Sleepily she replied: "Can you believe my husband's out golfing in that?"

AN Airdrie Golf Club member told us that she once phoned *The Herald*'s sports desk with the competition results of the ladies section, which included who had won the May Cup. It appeared in the paper as the Makeup winner.

TWENTY-ONE medals belonging to the late Rangers star Bobby Shearer are being auctioned this week. We remember a reader chatting to Bobby at Green's Playhouse in the 1960s when a wee Glasgow wummin demanded of Bobby: "Hey you, lift up your trouser legs."

Continued our reader: "He asked why and the wee wummin, who had, it's fair to say, imbibed somewhat, explained, 'Every time ma man comes in wi' a drink in him, he says ah've got legs like Bobby Shearer, an' ah want tae see whit they look like.'"

CONGRATULATIONS on the American women's football team winning the World Cup. As American Samantha Ruddy commented: "Man, for a country that doesn't care about women or soccer, we are bloody amazing at women's soccer."

ENJOYING the Wimbledon coverage? As our old colleague Ruth Wishart commented: "One of the penalties of watching Wimbledon in Scotland is seeing folk in sundresses whilst idly wondering whether you can justify putting the heating on for an hour or two."

RETIRED referee Brian McGinley once told of officiating at an Aberdeen–Rangers game where Aberdeen were winning

1–0, and with just a minute to go it had descended into a melee with players pushing and shoving each other.

Rather than resort to a series of red cards he blew for full time with furious Rangers manager Jock Wallace following him up the tunnel and demanding to know why he was in such a rush.

Trying to diffuse the situation, Brian told him he had to get to a wedding. "Is it your mother and father's?" bellowed Jock.

A POSTSCRIPT to the Arsenal signing of Celtic defender Kieran Tierney, which many Celtic fans were unhappy about. As one supporter of the green-and-white declared on social media: "Scared tae drink this weekend in case I have a full-blown breakdown in front of folk, and start greetin' about Kieran Tierney leaving. Think I'll stay in, go for a big bubble bath and eat my bodyweight in ice cream. That's wit the birds dae when they are getting over blokes, innit?"

GREAT football from the Scotland women's team until they were brought down by a very dodgy referee and VAR technology. Actually, not everyone blamed the referee.

As our old colleague Stewart Weir declared: "If it hadn't been for John Logie Baird inventing television, we wouldn't have had VAR. Scotland only has itself to blame . . ."

If you missed the game, Scotland had taken a 3–0 lead against Argentina but due to the astonishing decision by the ref to allow Argentina to retake a saved penalty, they drew 3–3 to go out of the tournament.

As a Celtic fan summed it up for us: "Scotland men's team: 'We've invented every possible way to mentally exit a tournament.' Scotland's women: 'Hold our Bacardi Breezers.'"

SPECULATION continues on where Motherwell's £3-million star David Turnbull will turn up after turning down Celtic's initial signing bid. Junior football side Maryhill FC took to social media this week to announce: "Feel the need to clarify something. We have been asked repeatedly if David Turnbull has snubbed Celtic for Maryhill. Yes and no. We are currently in talks with Turnbull, but not the same one. Our David Turnbull is a goalie, 42 years old, 18 and a half stone and loves rolls 'n' chips as well as cans of Vimto."

Incidentally, Maryhill FC, who play in a neat wee park tucked away behind Maryhill Road, were also appealing for anyone with a spare grass strimmer to get in touch so we don't think they were throwing away anything like £3-million to sign their David Turnbull.

SEXISM it seems is still alive and well in our Scottish golf courses. Norman McLean in Ayr tells us: "As four ladies appeared walking up the 18th fairway pushing their electric caddy cars, a member remarked, looking from the clubhouse window and in a lovely north accent, 'Ah here comes the battery hens.'"

SO, Scotland lost to Belgium, but it wasn't the horror story it has been in the past. Nevertheless, our old chum and colleague Stewart Weir observed: "Forget that VAR stuff – Scotland conceded the first goal because some players went to sleep. The only technology that would have saved us was an alarm clock."

But perhaps the pithiest comment from the Euro qualifiers was from Ireland manager Mick McCarthy, who, when asked why the team arrived late, said: "The bus broke down." Asked by a journalist to expand on that, he said: "It wouldn't go any further."

A READER tells us about a retired woman visiting her doctor who is asked about her activity levels and she tells him: "Well just yesterday I took a four-hour walk through some pretty rough terrain. I must have pushed my way through a mile of brambles, got sand in my shoes and my eyes, and climbed several rocky hills. I even had to go to the bathroom behind some big trees. But I had a couple of glasses of wine at the end of it."

"A keen hiker?" asked the doctor.

"No, just a terrible golfer," she said.

THERE were many empty seats at the Europa League final the other night with many fans citing the distance, cost and difficulties of travelling to Baku for the game. A football fan phones The Diary to tell us: "Only a few Chelsea fans managed to make it to Azerbaijan. I heard one of them on the telly declare, 'This place don't look nuffin like the *Harry Potter* film.'"

FANTASTIC win by Liverpool the other night against Barcelona. It somehow reminds us of the Provost of Fife no less, Jim Leishman, the former footballer and manager who once spoke at a charity dinner in Glasgow and explained: "As a young player I could have signed for Liverpool, Manchester United, or Chelsea." Jim added after a pause: "But none of them wanted me, so I signed for Dunfermline."

LIVERPOOL'S Jurgen Klopp will be regarded as one of their greatest managers, alongside Scotland's Bill Shankly of course.

The book *Scottish Sporting Legends* told of Shankly berating forward Tony Hateley for his lack of talent. Defending himself, Tony declared: "You have to admit I'm great in the air."

But Shankly tartly replied: "I'll grant you that, son, but so was Douglas Bader, and he had two better legs than you'll ever have."

GROWING old, continued. Says a reader from Stirling: "Having played in the opening game of the new golf season a week past on Saturday and a couple of rounds since, I have to admit that it is becoming easier to get the ball out of a bunker than getting me out after playing the shot."

WE pass on the conversation with former Rangers star Ally McCoist who was asked on a sports radio show if his five sons, including Argyll and Arran, were named after the places where they were conceived. Ally tried to deny it, but when the presenter asked about his son Mitchell, Ally played along by saying: "There's a Mitchell Library in Glasgow – but you have to be very quiet!"

WE should, of course, also mention Junior Football. Our chum Graham Scott was at an Auchinleck Talbot vs Beith game in the old mining village when an Auchinleck fan, frustrated by a delay in the game, shouted: "C'mon ref, ah've ma work to get up for in the morning."

A Beith fan immediately shouted over: "You don't live in Auchinleck then?"

A DIARY story from a Kilmalcolm resident reminded a Milngavie reader of an incident in Kilmalcolm golf club's TV room. He tells us: "One of the club members went over to the hatch as it was then, to order a round of drinks. Unfortunately, as he leant into the hatch to catch the barman's attention, he passed wind very loudly. One of his pals asked, 'Bell not working again, Davie?'"

WE mentioned the number of locals who were watching the Auchinleck Talbot vs Ayr United Scottish Cup tie from their bedroom windows overlooking the ground even though it was live on BBC Scotland. An Ayrshire reader gets in touch with the explanation: "Just been told the reason was they thought the satellite dish for beaming the game live was in fact the television detector van."

A POSTSCRIPT to the Scotland–Israel match at Hampden with Barrie Crawford telling us: "My son took a group of BB Junior Section boys to the match. It was one wee lad's first time at a live game. After about five minutes, the boy turned to my son and asked, 'What's happened to the commentary?'"

OUR story about annual meetings of small organisations reminded Foster Evans: "A leading auditor once told me about attending a bowling club AGM in Clydebank. The meeting was a bit unruly. The chairman called the meeting to order to hear the auditor's report by saying, 'This wee fat Tory has come all the way from Glasgow, so shut up and listen.'"

WAYWARD golf shots continued. Says John Robertson: "A good few years ago at Carnwath golf club, before they moved the green for the par three second hole away from the main road, a Carnwath player's tee shot bounced out on to the road. It then hit the service bus and bounced back into play and on to the green.

"His opponent made the obvious comments about luck, but the Carnwath player's response was, 'I knew the bus would be on time.'"

A MILNGAVIE golfer tells us that the golf club at Balmore, the village between Milngavie and Kirkintilloch, has won the local league for senior players for the first time. The euphoric members were joshing that perhaps they should hire an open-top bus to celebrate their success. A club member later came in and declared: "I contacted a local bus company who told me, 'We don't have much call for these buses up here in Scotland, sir.' The bus company guy then added, 'I think we once had a provisional booking from a Mr A. Salmond back in 2014 . . . but he never came back to us.'"

READER Bob Jamieson confesses: "My hearing is certainly not what it was. My wife and I were playing golf at Windyhill in Bearsden, following a group of Japanese businessmen. They teed off and one of them hit his ball way left, landing on our fairway. He wandered towards it, stopped in front of me, bowed and said, 'Ahoomabaw,' then played his shot. I turned to my wife and said, 'He just said something in Japanese, no idea what it meant.' My wife just looked at me and said, 'He hooked his ball.'"

GROWING old, continued. Says Jim Morrison: "At Erskine golf club last week, two of the older members were talking and one said, 'I'm thinking of giving up the golf, Donald – I can't reach the par fours in two any more.'

"His pal replied, 'Ye think that's bad? I've got trouble reaching the par threes in two.'"

WE often note folk who have a bit of fun with reviews on TripAdvisor. The latest we spotted was the Motherwell FC podcast team who, after Motherwell's victory against rivals Hamilton Accies, wrote a review of Hamilton's New Douglas Park: "Very accommodating, allowed us to leave with three points. Locals low in numbers and very quiet. Would visit again."

THE wit and wisdom of coaches and caddies can fill books. A reader told us of her aunt having lessons in St Andrews, and as she persisted with her increasingly wild, but energetic swing, the coach told her: "Hen, you're only trying tae move a wee ba' – no a graun' piana."

And impersonator Rory Bremner recalled playing at St Andrews where he hit the ball into a huge bush. His impassive caddy remarked: "Ye could wrap that up in bacon, sir, and Lassie'd no find it."

THE late Bishop John Mone of Paisley loved his golf, and once joked at the annual golf competition between Catholic priests and Church of Scotland ministers that he had told folk that he was going away on a course for handicapped clergy. He also explained his rule of thumb that if your golf handicap was higher than eight then you were neglecting your golf. If it was lower than eight you were neglecting your parish.

GOLF can turn many players into philosophers. One keen golfer told us the truism: "If your opponent has trouble remembering whether he took a six or a seven, he probably took an eight."

FORMER US President Bill Clinton was guest speaker at the Scottish Business Awards when he was making a point about the level of surveillance in our lives by explaining how everyone now has camera phones. So, he asked the question: "Do you know the difference between when I played golf at St Andrews today and when I played there ten years ago?" He perhaps wasn't expecting the Scottish businessman who shouted out: "Ten shots?"

WEBSITE Football Scotland has been asking if football fans are dealt with more strictly than rugby fans when it comes to stewarding and policing. Among the football fans who responded was a Partick Thistle supporter who said: "Stewards took my favourite juice cup away when I was seven."

Another attending a Celtic game recalled: "At Parkhead I got screamed at to sit in my seat which was non-existent. I had to crouch and pretend to sit so I didn't get thrown out."

And our favourite: "Just when the headset mics came in, I asked the polis going into Airdrie vs Morton if he was trying to be Madonna. Needless to say, I waited in the pub for the bus back."

WELL, did you watch the World Darts Championship final on the telly? It does seem a little strange that such a mundane game has gripped the attention of so many people. As Irish bookmakers Paddy Power commented with a truism after the dramatic semi-final game between Michael Smith and Nathan Aspinall: "It's matches like this that inspire you to go down the pub and throw a few darts yourself. Then your first three darts total up to seven and you can't hit a double to save your life, so f**k it, stick to five-a-side."

IT was our feature writer colleague on *The Herald*, Teddy Jamieson, who got to the bottom of the oft-told tale of flash Charlie Nicholas, when at Celtic in the late 1970s, tearing up a £20 note in front of a fan who was giving him grief, to show he was rich and didn't care.

Teddy asked Charlie about it who said: "I think I was 17, 18. I shouldn't have been allowed in the pub. There was this guy giving me earache all night. 'I'm better than you. I'm better than you.' I went into the Gents and he was right at my back and he gave it to me again. So, I took the £20 and said, 'Can you do this?' I ripped it up and threw it on the ground and walked out. He came out and went to his mates looking a bit sheepish. My point was made and I sprinted straight back into the toilet to get the £20 note to sellotape it up."

CELTIC fans were in shock that manager Brendan Rodgers would ditch them to manage mid-table English side Leicester City. In Ayrshire Matt Vallance heard a Kilmarnock fan pass on the news to a Celtic-supporting mate who insisted that, "It was just paper talk." But the Kilmarnock fan memorably insisted: "If you think that, you're clutching at more straws than a scarecrow playing wi' himsel'."

Anyway, we turn to social media where a Celtic fan explains the situation: "Rodgers moaned for a new pitch costing millions, then he does this. Reminds me of that time ma Auntie Liz moaned for a new suite and ma Uncle Davie got wan oan HP, only for her to run away wae a wee guy fae the bowling club who had more money."